Helping Those Who Hurt

Books by

H. Norman Wright

FROM BETHANY HOUSE PUBLISHERS

The Complete Book of Christian Wedding Vows

A Dad-Shaped Hole in My Heart

Helping Those Who Hurt

Making Peace With Your Mom

H. NORMAN WRIGHT

Helping Those Who Hurt

BETHANY HOUSE PUBLISHERS

Minneapolis, Minnesota

Helping Those Who Hurt
Copyright © 2003, 2006
H. Norman Wright

Cover design by Josh Madison

Published by Bethany House Publishers
11400 Hampshire Avenue South
Bloomington, Minnesota 55438

Bethany House Publishers is a division of
Baker Publishing Group, Grand Rapids, Michigan.

Printed in the United States of America

ISBN-13: 978-0-7642-0306-0   ISBN-10: 0-7642-0306-1

The Library of Congress has cataloged the original edition as follows:

Wright, H. Norman.
    Helping those who hurt : reaching out to your friends in need / by H. Norman Wright.
        p. cm.
    Includes bibliographical references (p.).
    ISBN 0-7642-2742-4 (pbk.)
    1. Helping behavior-Religious aspects-Christianity. 2. Friendship-Religious aspects-Christianity. I. Title.
    BV464.H4W75 2003
    253-dc21

                                                                    2003001456

H. NORMAN WRIGHT is a licensed marriage, family, and child therapist and a certified trauma specialist. He serves on the faculty of Talbot School of Theology at Biola University and is former director of Biola University's Graduate Department of Marriage, Family, and Child Counseling. He is the bestselling author of more than seventy books, including *Communication: Key to Your Marriage, Quiet Times for Couples,* and *Always Daddy's Girl.* Norm and his wife, Joyce, have been married for forty-seven years and currently live in Bakersfield, California.

Contents

Called to Help a Friend

CHAPTER 1

IN ONE SMALL EUROPEAN VILLAGE was a town square that held a special statue. This statue was the pride and joy of the small town, but World War II arrived and soon the bombs began falling on the town. One day the statue was hit and blown to pieces. The residents collected all the shattered pieces and slowly did what they could to re-create it. When they finished the reconstruction of their beloved statue of Jesus, they noticed that the only pieces missing were the hands. So they placed a plaque at the base of the statue with the words *Now we are the only hands that Jesus has.*

Isn't this our calling to those around us? We are His hands. You may have the desire to reach out and help your friends but hesitate. "What do I say? What do I do? What should I avoid?" You're not alone with your concern. You don't want to say or do the wrong thing and hurt your friends. And during a loss or crisis you can't rely on them to tell you what they need. They may not know or have the energy it takes to tell you.

What will you say when a friend comes to you and says:

"I've just been told I have cancer and it's terminal."

"It was a phone call . . . he's dead . . . he's been killed . . . my husband."

"My daughter just told me she's been molested for three years."

"I was in the video store and it was robbed! The gun went off. I can't even think."

"I went to school to pick up my son. He wasn't there. They say he was kidnapped."

"My husband just told me he wants a divorce. I'm shocked. I didn't know anything was wrong."

I was sitting at the kitchen table in my daughter's home, looking through a magazine, while Sheryl fed her six-month-old daughter. The phone rang and she answered the call while continuing to feed her daughter. When she said, "Oh, no. I'm so sorry to hear that. That must have been a shock," my ears perked up. I continued to listen and watch her facial expressions. It was apparent that her friend was in some kind of distress. I observed Sheryl while she listened and reflected back what she was hearing. She made statements like, "So you found the evidence, and that's what led you to confront him," and "You're sounding hurt and disappointed." From time to time she asked questions: "Which of the children are aware of this?" and "How will _____ handle this at her stage in life?" She also asked, "Had you thought about this possibility?" and "Have you considered this?"

When her friend wasn't sure or seemed to waver, Sheryl said, "Is that really your responsibility at this time, or is it his?" She helped her friend reconsider what was best to do and encouraged her to take the necessary steps. "You've given him more than a chance and trusted his word. Now it's been broken. I think you'll know what to do." She helped her friend explore several options as well as the consequences. On several occasions she reflected and clarified while her friend was thinking out loud. I could tell just from my daughter's comments and facial expressions that her friend was fairly devastated. I thought it was good that this woman had a trusted friend to talk with and help her work through this life-changing event.

My daughter wasn't judgmental in any way but assisted her in clarifying the problem. After Sheryl hung up the phone, she made the comment,

"I'm sure glad I'm not a counselor. I wouldn't want to do this for a living." I smiled and said, "Oh, sure. You've only done this for fifteen years as a manicurist. You've helped as many women as some counselors have while you were sitting there doing their nails." She laughed because she knew it was true. She helped many who would never go talk to a counselor or pastor. But they would listen to her because of some of her own life experiences, her listening, her insight, and her desire to help. And so can you.

After forty years of counseling I'm convinced that as many as one-third to one-half of all the people I've seen didn't need to come and see me. That is, they wouldn't have needed to see me if they'd had a trained pastor, lay caregiver, or knowledgeable friend to meet with. I'm all for professional counseling when it's needed, but many issues can be resolved with the help of a friend who is willing to learn how to minister to others. And as Christians it is not an option to help or not help others. That is what the Christian life is all about—ministering to others.

If you are saying, "I wouldn't know what to say or do," there is a solution. Just imagine what our churches would be like if people knew what to say and do as well as what *not* to say and do! This can happen. This needs to happen. If others have no one to help them, no one to talk with, they end up talking to themselves. And the advice and help they give themselves isn't the best.

Many years ago I was on the staff of a church as minister of education and youth. A man by the name of Alan Loy McGinnis was attending our church while completing his graduate work. Since he was also a minister, he would preach from time to time in the evening service. One Sunday night he walked up to the pulpit and said, "Tonight I would like to share with you what to say, what not to say, what to do, and what not to do at a time of bereavement."

Ours was not a note-taking congregation . . . until that moment. As I sat on the platform I could see people reaching for offering envelopes, prayer request cards, or any other piece of paper they could find to write on. I still have my notes from that evening. It was the first (and unfortunately the last) time I've ever heard a message on how to help another person at a time of need. Those in attendance that evening left with a greater sense of confidence on how to help another person.

You'll be more likely to reach out if you know what to say.

It's true—helping a hurting person *is* a bit scary. We want to do the right thing, not the wrong thing—say what will help, not what will hurt. To add to our confusion, our friend is "not quite herself." She's different. We want our friend fixed and back to normal.

All you have to do is care. Harold Ivan Smith described the process so well:

> *Grief sharers always look for an opportunity to actively care. You can never "fix" an individual's grief, but you can wash the sink full of dishes, listen to him or her talk, take his or her kids to the park. You can never "fix" an individual's grief but you can visit the cemetery with him or her.*
>
> *Grief sharing is not about fixing—it's about showing up. Coming alongside. Being interruptible. "Hanging out" with the bereaving. In the words of World War II veterans, "present and reporting for duty."*
>
> *The grief path is not a brief path. It's a marathon, not a sprint.[1]*

What can you expect from a friend who is hurting? Actually, not very much. And the more her experience moves beyond a loss and closer to a crisis or trauma, the more this is true. Sometimes you'll see a friend experiencing a case of the "crazies." Her response seems irrational. She's not herself. Her behavior is different from or even abnormal compared to the person not going through a major loss. Just remember, she's reacting to an out-of-the-ordinary event. What she *experienced* is abnormal, so her *response* is actually quite normal. If what the person has experienced is traumatic she may even seem to exhibit some of the symptoms of ADD (Attention Deficit Disorder). And because your friend is this way, she is *not* to be avoided. Others are needed at this time in her life. These are responses you *can* expect. Your friend is no longer functioning as she once did—and probably won't for a while.

You Are Needed

You are needed when a person experiences a sudden intrusion or disruption in her life. If you (or another friend) aren't available, the only person she has to talk with for guidance, support, and direction is herself. And who wants support from someone struggling with a case of the "crazies"?

But a problem may arise when your friend doesn't realize that she needs you, at least at that *particular time.* Your sensitivity is needed at this point. Remember, when your friend is hurting and facing a loss, you are dealing with a loss as well, because the relationship you had with your friend has changed. It's not the same. It's no longer equal. You may feel as though you're the giver and your friend is the taker. The sharing the two of you had before has changed. The give-and-take you used to experience has vanished. What's important to you does not seem important to your friend. Your life and experiences have taken a backseat to the devastating experience of your friend.

You can't put a time limit on your role as a helper or giver. This may get old for you, especially when it stretches on for months. Remember that when your relationship gets back to normal, it will be a new normal. It won't be the same. Sometimes a hurting friend ends up feeling both resentful over being dependent upon you and at the same time appreciative of all you've done for her.

Your friend in mourning—though he doesn't perceive himself that way—is self-centered. You simply cannot exist for him as a whole person, probably for a very long time. This can be hard on relationships. Friends get weary of ceasing to be perceived as human beings with feelings and problems and hopes in their own right. They get weary of being there for the other person in seemingly a one-sided relationship. But suffice it to say that your friend in mourning will not be able to empathize with you about things involving you for many months—or maybe years.[2]

What Can You Do?

You can listen even when she's not talking. Sometimes she's not able to talk, but your attentive presence lets your friend know you're there to listen. You let her know you want to hear her story when she's up to talking about it.

If your friend is devastated and coming apart at the seams or sitting there stunned, you can't make her feel better or fix her. When we try it's often to help us feel useful and relieve our anxiety about seeing someone in this state. Remember, you can never be all you want to be or all your friend wants you to be for her.[3]

You will be hurt at times since some of what you offer or do will be rejected. Because you haven't experienced the same loss, she may feel uncomfortable with you while at the same time want your help. In your heart and mind give her permission not to be as she was. If something is said or done that offends you, remind yourself that your friend cannot be expected to be as she was. You may wonder, *Did I say something wrong? Am I off base?* The answer is no. You're dealing with unpredictability. You're all right.

You may be tempted at times to set your friend straight spiritually. You might hear statements like, "I thought I could count on God, but even

He let me down" or "How could a loving God let something like that happen?" or "I think I'm losing my faith in God. I can't even pray anymore." Squelch your desire to start quoting Bible verses, shove a book in her face, or try to give answers. Be glad you're hearing where she is spiritually. Respond with a simple "Yes, what's happened doesn't make much sense, does it? It's hard to understand. I wish I had an answer for you," or just listen and reflect.

There will be times when your friend doesn't want you around. If you sense that might be the case, ask her, "What would be more comfortable for you at this time: for me to be here with you or to give you some space? I can do either." If your presence isn't needed, say, "I'll check back with you another time to see what I can do to assist you."

I will make this statement several times in this book: The best support you can give your friend is to *normalize her feelings*. This simply means reassuring her that what she is experiencing is natural; she isn't crazy. This advice can provide the greatest relief of all. But it means *you* need to understand what someone experiences from a loss or a trauma. (This will be discussed in chapter 7.)

Biblical Guidelines for Helping

How can you help a friend? There are many elements involved. In Proverbs 3:5–6 we are instructed to "Lean on, trust in, and be confident in the Lord with all your heart and mind and do not rely on your own insight or understanding. In all your ways know, recognize, and acknowledge Him, and he will direct and make straight and plain your paths" (AMP).

With all their years of training and experience, professional counselors frequently wonder what they should do or say. This experience prompts all of us to go back to the Lord and ask, "Lord, what should I do now? What does this person need?" You'll find yourself there time and time again. If you begin to assist and help your friend out of your own strength, mistakes will be made. We all need to rely upon the power and wisdom of God.

Helping others includes experiencing genuine interest and love for the individual. We can listen and rely upon the power of God for knowing how to respond, but we must also have a genuine interest and love. If it's not there, you can't fake it, and your friend will know if you are. Proverbs 27:9: "Oil and perfume rejoice the heart; so does the sweetness of a friend's counsel that comes from the heart" (AMP). It's so easy to rattle off an answer that's superficial and doesn't meet your friend's need. We have to ask ourselves, "How do I really feel about this individual who is coming to me? Am I genuinely concerned? If not, maybe I should pray about my own attitude. Perhaps I'm not the one to try to help." You will be drawn to help some you know and not others. It could be their problems are beyond you; maybe they overwhelm you or activate some unresolved issues in your own life.

To help someone else, you need to know when to speak and when enough has been said. Proverbs 10:19 emphasizes this principle: "In a multitude of words transgression is not lacking, but he who restrains his lips is prudent" (AMP). This is a sign of an individual who has knowledge. He chooses his words well. "Even fools seem to be wise if they keep quiet; if they don't speak, they appear to understand" (17:28 NCV).

Proverbs 29:20: "Do you see a man who is hasty in his words? There is more hope for a [self-confident] fool than for him" (AMP). Being hasty means you just go ahead and blurt out what you're thinking without considering the consequences, the effect it will have on others. If you're an extrovert, you probably need to talk to think something through. Extroverts tend to talk first and then realize what they've said. But this is a time to hold back and get your thoughts in order. When you are ministering to a hurting friend and she shares something that shocks you, don't feel that you have to respond immediately. I've heard people respond to their hurting friend, "You did *what*?" Take a few moments to pray, asking God to give you the words. Then try to formulate what you want to say.

If you don't know what to say, one of the best things to do is ask for more information: "Tell me some more about it" or "Give me some more background." This gives you more time. You don't have to come right out and say something. There may be times when you say, "I need a few seconds to go through what you said and decide what to share at this time." This takes the pressure off you and also off your friend.

Timing is another important principle. Proverbs 15:23: "A man has joy in making an apt answer, and a word spoken at the right moment—how good it is!" (AMP). The correct answer spoken at the right moment is needed.

Keeping confidences is foundational. Can you keep a confidence when somebody shares something with you? Proverbs 20:19: "Gossips can't keep secrets, so avoid people who talk too much" (NCV). If you have a friend who is a gossiper, who can't keep something hidden, the Scripture is saying, Watch out! Don't associate with that person too much. Proverbs 21:23: "He who guards his mouth and his tongue keeps himself from troubles" (AMP).

Most of us, when we have had something shared with us, have had the temptation to share it with others—even a confidence from a friend. And the more shocking it is, the more we're tempted to share. But such conversation is a violation of trust and friendship; tremendous damage is done by sharing confidences. What we must do as a Christian and as a friend is ask God to help us bury confidential information deep inside or give it away to the Lord so that it will not come out, either on purpose or through some subconscious motivation. Does your friend want you to share this issue with anyone else, including family? Ask her. (If she's highly suicidal or homicidal you will have to get some assistance.)

Another passage reflects the idea of sensitive understanding. Proverbs 25:20: "Singing songs to someone who is sad is like taking away his coat on a cold day or pouring vinegar on soda" (NCV). Being merry or joyful around the person who is deeply hurting and suffering, and making inappropriate comments or jokes, even statements such as, "Oh, you really don't feel that way, snap out of it," is inappropriate. Your friend hurts so much she's unable to focus on what is happening. And such inappropriate statements or jokes can add to her pain.

So how do you give good advice? If you give suggestions, give tentative ones. "What if you did . . . ?" "Have you ever considered . . . ?" "What possibilities have you come up with?" It's safest when giving advice to offer several alternatives. Don't say to a person, "This is exactly what you need to do." If you do, you are assuming the responsibility for the solution. If your suggestion doesn't work, she may come back and say, "You really gave me a stupid idea. It didn't work. It's your fault." Giving several tentative suggestions not only is safer for you, but enables your friend to think it through for herself. Most people have the ability to resolve their problems, but they need the encouragement to do it.

One way to help a friend is to gently confront her when you see her heading down the wrong path. Confrontation is not an attack on another person if given gently and sensitively. This is important because she may already be feeling guilty and ashamed, and experiencing what she sees as judgment or condemnation will likely make her feel rejected.

So confront someone only when you have genuine empathy for her. A confrontation should be an act of grace. It's done to reveal discrepancies or distortions in someone's intended direction or thinking. Confrontation is also used to challenge the underdeveloped and the unused skills and resources of your friend.

Your purpose in confronting your friend should be to help her make better decisions for herself, become more accepting of where she is in life, and be less destructive and more productive. "Wounds from a friend can be trusted, but an enemy multiplies kisses" (Proverbs 27:6).

But you cannot use the same approach for every person; you must be sensitive to her individual needs. Adaptability is important. "And we earnestly beseech you, brethren, admonish (warn and seriously advise) those who are out of line ... encourage the timid and fainthearted, help and give your support to the weak souls, [and] be very patient with everybody [always keeping your temper]" (1 Thessalonians 5:14 AMP).

How do you confront? Not with anger or with a statement. You may want to point out that what someone's doing is irresponsible or even dumb, but you'll offend and even sever the relationship. Your friend needs to hear care and concern in your voice; confrontation can be made in a tentative manner with statements such as, "I wonder if . . ." "Could it be . . . ?" "Is it possible . . . ?" "Does this make sense to you?" and "How do you react to this perception?" With your questions, *lead* her to where you want her to go. Practice these questions out loud again and again until they're a part of your helping reservoir of information and approach.

Another principle we find in the Word of God is edification. Some of these passages might be familiar to you. Galatians 6:2 teaches the concept of bearing one another's burdens. Romans 14:19 reads, "So let us then definitely aim for and eagerly pursue what makes for harmony and for mutual upbuilding (edification and development) of one another" (AMP). The word *edify,* which is part of helping, means to hold up or to promote growth in Christian wisdom, grace, virtue, and holiness. Our helping includes edification. We have to ask ourselves, "Is what I'm sharing with that person going to cause her to grow in the Christian life and assist her to be strong?" A friend might come to you and say, "I really want you to help me." But what does she mean by *help?* She might mean agreeing with her point of view, or even taking her side. That is where you get into difficulty—taking sides.

Another way of helping others is encouragement. Proverbs 12:25: "Anxiety in a man's heart weighs it down, but an encouraging word makes it glad" (AMP). First Thessalonians 5:11: "Therefore encourage (admonish, exhort) one another and edify (strengthen and build up) one another, just as you are doing" (AMP).

The *American Heritage Dictionary* has one of the better definitions of *encourage*. It's a "tendency or disposition to expect the best possible outcome, or to dwell on the most hopeful aspect of a situation." When this is your attitude or perspective, you'll be able to encourage others. Encouragement is recognizing the other person as having worth and dignity. It means paying attention to her when she is sharing with you.

Hebrews 10:25 says, "Let us encourage one another." The word here means to keep someone on her feet who, if left to herself, would collapse. Your encouragement serves like the concrete pilings of a structural support.

Involvement and empathy are the scriptural basis for helping. Empathy is one of the most important commodities for helping. It's viewing the situation through your friend's eyes, feeling as she feels. The scriptural admonition to bear one another's burdens in Galatians 6:2 and to rejoice with those who rejoice and weep with those who weep in Romans 12:15 is what we call empathy.

It involves discrimination—to be able to get inside the other person, to look at the world through her perspective or frame of reference, and to get a feeling for what her world is like. Not only is it the ability to discriminate, but also to communicate to your friend this understanding in such a manner that she realizes you have picked up her feelings and behavior. We must be able to see with her eyes what her world is like. It is like being able to see another person's joy, to understand what underlies that joy, and to communicate this understanding to the person. Can you do this? Yes, you can learn. Be patient with yourself and with others.

Be open to God's leading, and may the words of a man who gave his life for others on 9/11 guide you:

Lord, take me where You want me to go,
Let me meet whom You want me to meet.
Help me to say what You want me to say.
And keep me from getting in Your way!
    —Father Mychal Judge[a]

The Miserable Comforters in Your Friend's Life

IF AN ENEMY WERE INSULTING ME, I could endure it; if a foe were raising himself against me, I could hide from him. But it is you, a man like myself, my companion, my close friend, with whom I once enjoyed sweet fellowship as we walked with the throng at the house of God" (Psalm 55:12–14).

There is one additional source of pain your friend will need to contend with—other people who make statements that hurt rather than console, hinder rather than comfort, and prolong the pain rather than relieve it. These people are *secondary wounders*. They'll give unwanted and bad advice as well as improperly applied Scripture. They're all around, even at church, and your friend won't be the first to experience this. Remember Job?

> *[Job] had four well-meaning but insufferable friends who came over to cheer him up and try to explain [his suffering]. They said that anybody with enough sense to come in out of the rain knew that God was just. They said that anybody old enough to spell his own name knew that since God was just, he made bad things happen to bad people and good things happen to good people. They said that such being the case, you didn't need a Harvard diploma to figure out that since bad things had happened to Job, then* ipso facto *he must have done something bad himself. But Job hadn't, and he said so, and*

that's not all he said either. "Worthless physicians are you all,"
he said. "Oh that you would keep silent, and it would be your
wisdom" (Job 13:4–5). They were a bunch of theological
quacks, in other words, and the smartest thing they could do
was shut up. But they were too busy explaining things to listen.[1]

Words Better Left Unsaid

Expect people to make statements that your friend would rather not hear. It will be difficult for her to respond to these people the way she would like to because of her state of grief or trauma. Perhaps others would learn not to make such insensitive statements if someone spoke up and said, "That's not true and it's not helpful. If you want to be helpful, I would appreciate it if you would . . ." But sometimes we excuse what these people say as "well-meaning," which is questionable. Oftentimes they're just reflecting their own anxieties, fears, or lack of having dealt with issues in their own lives.

Let your friend know she can anticipate at least three common reactions from the people she confides in.

The Inability of Others to Accept the Bad News

There are numerous reasons for the inability to accept bad news, but the results are the same: People can't handle the situation or accept the person who has created the problem.

Often people will verbalize sympathy and support, but their attitude and behavior communicates rejection. Your hurting friend will wonder which message to believe. Remind her that when other people are uncomfortable with a situation, their nonverbal responses are saying, "I want you 'normal' as soon as possible, or at least acting that way." But your friend can't and won't be "normal" for some time, and no one else can determine how she should respond to her tragedy and loss.

The more others hear about your friend's difficulties, the greater the level of their discomfort; they don't want her discomfort invading their lives. So they may distance themselves. When people react badly to your friend, it may help to explain some of the adjustments they are experiencing. The person who is hurting could tell others she understands how uncomfortable they may feel learning about this. Don't expect them to open up and say they're having difficulty with the situation. They probably won't. But if she admits her struggle with her mixture of feelings, at least others may feel more comfortable with her, whether they admit anything or not.

Unsolicited Advice

Everyone is an expert or knows of a similar case, and since those who care want to help, they give emphatic suggestions about steps that should be taken. Sometimes they're offended if your friend doesn't show enthusiasm and indicate she's going to follow their advice immediately.

Your friend can thank them for their concern and suggestions and let them know they are adding to the wealth of information she's been gathering, but she shouldn't commit to taking their advice.

Overwhelmed With Help

Yet another reaction, especially from people who really care, will be to overwhelm your friend with help. I've seen relatives and friends invade a family's boundaries and actually take away their decision-making opportunities. Your friend needs help in determining how much assistance she wants and establishing boundaries with any intrusive friends or relatives.

A good starting point for your friend is to make a list of her needs and questions and then list the type of outside help she's looking for. It's all right to take time to think, pray, and consider the options and the consequences of each. She doesn't need to let others pressure or rush her into anything.[2]

What Not to Say

Listen to these firsthand experiences of being wounded by others:

My first day back to work after my mother's funeral, a co-worker said, "I know just how you feel. My cat died recently." How could someone compare my mother's major role in my life with a cat? It would have been more sensitive to simply say, "I'm sorry."[3]

Our young daughter, who was dying from leukemia, loved to read. When we took her to the ophthalmologist for a new pair of glasses, he said, "She's going to die soon anyway. Don't waste your money on a new prescription." He didn't understand that dying children need to make every day count and live to the fullest the life they have left.[4]

My son, who had Down's syndrome, died when he was twenty years old. A relative said, "What a blessing. He is better off now." I wondered if her twenty-two-year-old son would be "better off" if he were dead and if that would bless her. Does an IQ make one life worth more than another? Does an IQ change a mother's grief? I had cared for my precious, loving son his entire life, and I desperately missed him and his daily hugs. Many thought I would be relieved. Very few people understood my loss, and I felt very alone in my grieving.[5]

Following my miscarriage, people would say, "At least you have other children" or "God probably took the baby because there was something wrong with it" or "At least you are healthy and will probably conceive again." After my grandfather died, my grandmother told me that friends said, "At least you had all those years together." Don't say AT LEAST. Don't try to mini-mize someone's pain. It only insults the griever.[6]

Not only will there be comments that hurt but responses such as with-drawal. Your friend may wonder if she's contracted the plague. One insightful individual said:

You feel so isolated within yourself. When people withdraw from you because of their own discomfort, in a way, it's almost like an accusation that you were at fault. You feel you must have done something wrong, or this wouldn't be happening to you. On the other hand, you almost feel like they don't want to be around you because they feel it might be catching. I know people don't know what to say. I would rather they'd come and be with me or ask permission, "Would you like someone to be with you?" rather than feel, "Well, I don't know what to say so I think I'll stay away."

Perhaps you've experienced this yourself. If so, you know this pain of rejection.

Over the years I've heard so many inappropriate remarks that intensify the hurt and grief. The following examples are given as a guide of what *not* to say.

"I don't understand why you're still crying. Life goes on, you know."

"Look, you only lost your stepfather. What about your mother? She has a greater loss than you and she's pulled herself together."

"No one should feel that way about losing a cat. It's only an animal. You can find another one."

"This will make your family closer. It's an opportunity to grow together."

"Don't you appreciate what you have left?"

"Next time we'll be sure not to use that doctor or hospital."

"You've started out in new jobs before, so just look at this layoff as a great opportunity like George did when he got fired."

"You shouldn't feel that way. After all, you have the Lord."

"The past needs to be put behind us. Let's move on to the future with God."

"At least he didn't suffer."

"Well, just be glad it wasn't your only child."

"Look at it this way. Losing your husband this young and without children will make it easier for you to handle."

"The children need you to be strong."

"This must be God's will."

Statements like these don't help or comfort. They only intensify the person's feelings of loss and despair.

Sometimes people take an "It could have been worse" approach to their grieving friend in the hope of lessening the hurt. Unfortunately, at this point in time it doesn't work. In *The Survival Guide for Widows*, the author describes this approach:

> *I have one friend who, whenever we got together, at one point would nod her head wisely and say sententiously, "There are worse things than death." It was home-truth time, and she wanted me to know how lucky I was that I didn't have a living vegetable tied up to tubes in the hospital, or a human skeleton wasting away with pain in front of my eyes. I know, I know. We are given enough strength, I hope, to bear our own pain. I would not trade with others, nor they with me, in all likelihood. ... But the widow doesn't feel very lucky and resents being reminded that she still owes a debt of gratitude. She'll come around to it.[7]*

A mother who lost her child shared her painful experience:

All too common were the reminders. "You can have other babies," as if this baby were replaceable. "Don't get pregnant too soon. You don't want to replace this baby." Then they would add, "But be glad you can have others."

People say things to console themselves. There is no need to try to say things to make you feel better because there is not a thing they can say—not a word, not a phrase—that will make you feel better about your loss.

Her last statement is full of insight and wisdom. You can't take your friend's pain away. You can't fix others. Neither can I. None of us is the Great Healer.

Erin Linn compiled and categorized some of the painful and glib clichés that are thrown about so easily:

"Be Strong" Clichés

Big boys don't cry.
You must be strong for the children.
Support groups are for wimps.
Others have held up well. You can too.
No sense crying over spilled milk.
This is nature's way.

"Hurry Up" Clichés

You're not your old self.
Time will heal.
You're young, and you will be able to make a new life for yourself.
I just don't understand your behavior.
Life goes on.
No sense dwelling on the past.

"Guilt" Clichés

If you look around, you can always find someone who is worse off than yourself.

This is the work of the devil (which means that if you had a closer relationship with God, the devil could not have had his way).

Count your blessings.

Only the good die young.

Think of all your precious memories.

It's a blessing.

"God" Clichés

God needs him more than you do.

He is happy now, because he's with God.

God did this to show how powerful He can be in your life.

It was God's will.

God never gives us more than we can handle.

God helps those who help themselves.

"Discount" Clichés

I know just how you feel.

If there is anything I can do, just call me.

You can have more children.

It's better to have loved and lost than never to have loved at all.

Be glad you don't have a problem like mine.

What you don't know, won't hurt you.[8]

The Extent of Pain

What makes it so bad is that some of the worst comments come from well-intentioned acquaintances. A mother once said: "Someone told me it's probably a good thing she did die, so she wouldn't suffer. It tore me up for someone to say it was a good thing for a child to die. They haven't been there themselves. Another said, 'Maybe it's a good thing she died, because when she got older, she might have gotten into all kinds of trouble.'"

Statements of this nature merely added to the existing pain.

An all-too-common remark made to parents of children with cancer or a mentally handicapped child is, "You must be a special person, and God must really love you to give you a child like this."

Is this what a parent feels? As one mother said, "I'm not special; I don't want to do this either. In essence she's saying, 'God would never pick me for such things because I'm not strong.' I'm not that strong. And if I were, I'd rather my child was well or normal."

And then you get the medical "experts," who give unsolicited advice about chemotherapy. They'll say, "I wouldn't give her that stuff; people die from that." Parents struggle making decisions anyway—it's an overwhelming responsibility. But then you have people who don't know anything about it question you. Parents would rather hear, "What helped you come to that decision?" or "That must have been a hard decision to make."

One of the best ways I've discovered to help someone explain her situation and her needs is to write and photocopy a letter she can give to relatives, friends, acquaintances, and anyone else who asks. The letter states what has happened, what it will be like for her and her family, what others can expect, and what they can do for the person. By doing this, some of the pain is lessened by not having to tell the same story over and over—sometimes the repetition intensifies the pain.

Here's an example of a letter a family in crisis might write:

Dear friend,

You may have heard that we've had some difficulty with our oldest daughter. This has been very hard for my husband and me, and sometimes we're embarrassed over what has happened. Who would have expected that she would use drugs, leave high school, and live on the streets? The reason for this letter is that it's too painful to have to explain this over and over and over to our friends and relatives. We wish the problem would go away or we could just hide. But it doesn't and we can't, and we don't have any idea how this is going to turn out or when it will be over.

Please just keep asking how we're doing and continue to pray for us. We probably won't be the same each time you talk with us. We could be angry one time or depressed and dejected another time. Help us to talk, and just listen. If you have some suggestions, we will consider them, and perhaps something you say will benefit us.

You may find yourself with many questions as well as feelings too. You may be shocked and find yourself angry, wishing you could talk to our daughter and knock some sense into her head. You may even wonder, as we did, where we went wrong. What could we have done differently so this would not have happened? If you hear anyone judging us, please let them know we are already doing this and need their understanding.

Please don't withdraw from us. We need your support more than ever. Pray for us as well as our daughter. We want to continue to love her, encourage her, and believe in her. Pray that we won't just concentrate on our hurt but on her needs as well. Don't be surprised if we call you from time to time and say we need to talk, or ask you to go to dinner and talk about anything other than our daughter, since we need a break.

This is a loss to us and to our other children, and it's painful. Thank you for your support.

When your friend can take a positive, assertive step in reaching out to others and letting them know what she needs, she'll gain confidence and strength. She will feel less like a victim. Above all, she needs to talk about her feelings and concerns with family members. Encourage her to not try to protect them from the news, no matter what the problem, and to be aware of the danger of neglecting them because of all the attention given to the problem person.

Perhaps the words and advice of a hurting person summarize what's best not to do and what to do:

PLEASE

PLEASE, don't ask me if I'm over it yet.
I'll never be over it.

PLEASE, don't tell me she's in a better place.
She isn't here with me.

PLEASE, don't say at least she isn't suffering.
I haven't come to terms with why she had to suffer at all.

PLEASE, don't tell me you know how I feel
unless you have lost a child.

PLEASE, don't ask me if I feel better.
Bereavement isn't a condition that clears up.

PLEASE, don't tell me at least you had her for so many years.
What year would you choose for your child to die?

PLEASE, don't tell me God never gives us more than we can bear.

Helping Those Who Hurt

PLEASE, just say you are sorry.

PLEASE, just say you remember my child, if you do.

PLEASE, just let me talk about my child.

PLEASE, just let me cry.[9]

If You Want to Help, Listen

CHAPTER 3

IF YOU WANT TO HELP ANOTHER PERSON, just be there. Your presence does wonders. If you want to help another person, just listen. One of the greatest gifts one person can give to another is the gift of listening. It can be an act of love and caring. But far too many people in conversations only *hear* one another. Few actually *listen*.

Look at these verses from the Word of God. They tell us how God listens to us and how we should listen to others:

> *The eyes of the Lord are toward the righteous,*
> *And His ears are open to their cry.*
> *The face of the Lord is against evildoers,*
> *To cut off the memory of them from the earth.*
> *The righteous cry and the Lord hears,*
> *And delivers them out of all their troubles.*
> *The Lord is near to the brokenhearted,*
> *And saves those who are crushed in spirit.* (Psalm 34:15–18 NASB)

> *Let every man be quick to hear [a ready listener].* (James 1:19 AMP)

What Is Listening Really All About?

Listening means you're not thinking about what you're going to say when the other person stops talking. You are not busy formulating your response. You're concentrating on what is being said.

Listening means that you're completely accepting of what is being said, without judging what your friend is saying or how he is saying it. If you don't like his tone of voice or you can't condone what he's doing and you react on the spot, you may miss the meaning. Acceptance doesn't mean that you agree with the content of what he says; it means you acknowledge and understand that what he's saying is something he is feeling.

Listening means being able to repeat what your friend said and express what you think he is feeling while speaking to you. Real listening implies having a sincere interest in the other's feelings and opinions and attempting to understand those feelings from his perspective.

The word *hear* in the New Testament does not usually refer to an auditory experience. In most cases it means to *pay heed*. It requires tuning in to the right frequency.

Because of my retarded son, Matthew, who didn't have a vocabulary, I learned to listen with my eyes, reading the message in his nonverbal signals. This translated to my listening to what my counselees could not put into words. I learned to listen to the message behind the message—the hurt, ache, frustration, loss of hope, fear of rejection, feeling of betrayal, joy, delight, and the promise of change.

I also learned to reflect upon what I saw on another's face and in his posture, walk, and pace. Then I shared with him what I saw. This provided him an opportunity to explain further what he was thinking and feeling. He knew I was tuned in to him. Your friend needs to sense that you're in sync with him. Listen with your eyes to what he or she can't put into words.

Every message your friend shares has three parts: (1) the actual content, (2) the tone of voice, and (3) the nonverbal communication. It's possible to use the same word, statement, or question and express many different messages simply by changing tone of voice or body movement.

Nonverbal communication includes facial expression, body posture, and gestures or actions.

It's been suggested that successful communication consists of 7 percent content, 38 percent tone of voice, and 55 percent nonverbal communication. We're usually aware of the content of what we're saying, but not nearly as aware of our tone of voice.

When you say with the proper tone of voice, "I want to hear what you have to say," but then bury your head in paper work or check your watch, what is your friend to believe? When you ask, "How was your day?" in a flat tone while walking by him, what does he respond to—the verbal or nonverbal message?

Some people listen for facts, information, and details for their own use. Others listen because they feel sorry for the person. Your friend doesn't need this. On occasion, people listen out of obligation or necessity, or to be polite. If you do, your friend will pick this up. Some who listen are nothing more than voyeurs who have an incessant need to pry and probe into other people's lives. But some listen *because they care,* and this kind of listening provides unlimited opportunities for real ministry in people's lives. Listening that springs from caring builds closeness, reflects love, and is an act of grace. And this is what Jesus calls us to do.

Obstacles to Helpful Listening

There are four basic reasons why we listen to other people:

1. *To understand someone—a hurting person needs this.*
2. *To enjoy the other person—you may not enjoy him at this time.*
3. *To learn something from the one talking—you will, and it may shock you!*
4. *To give help, assistance, or comfort to the person—this is a major reason.*

The world is made up of many pseudolisteners who masquerade as the real product. But anyone who has listened for the above reasons does not *really* listen.

For caring listening to occur, we need to be aware of some of the common obstacles that can keep us from really hearing our hurting friends.

Defensiveness

You miss the message if your mind is busy thinking up a rebuttal, excuse, or exception to what your friend is saying.

There are a variety of defensive responses. Perhaps we *reach a premature conclusion.* "All right, I know just what you're going to say." Some who are in a crisis give you one sentence, become silent for a minute, then another sentence, then more silence. It could take him several minutes to complete a thought. Wait. Honor the pauses.

Two other defensive indicators may be *rehearsing our responses* and *responding to explosive words.*

Rehearsing a response (as well as other defensive postures) is not what Scripture calls us to do. Remember this verse: "Anyone who answers without listening is foolish and confused" (Proverbs 18:13 NCV).

Explosive words create an inner explosion of emotions. Not only do we react to explosive words, but we also may consciously choose to use some words that make it difficult for the other to hear. When you're reaching out to a hurting person, expect to hear thoughts, words, or phrases that you don't like, don't accept, or don't agree with.

Not all defensiveness is overtly expressed. Outwardly the hurting person could be agreeing, but inside he's saying just the opposite. Give him the opportunity to disagree with you. You're not there to convince him of something you believe.

Personal Biases

You may have a biased attitude toward certain people. It could be a person who speaks in a certain tone of voice or is from a certain ethnic group. Maybe it's someone of the opposite sex, or someone who reminds you of a person from your past. We all struggle with biases to some degree, and they will affect how well we listen.

It may be easier for you to listen to an angry person than to a sarcastic person; some tones or phrases may be enjoyable to listen to, while others may be annoying; the repetitive phrases a person uses (and may be unaware of) could bother you.

Some are distracted from listening because of gender. They're influenced by their expectations of what is appropriate for a man or woman to share or not share. The stereotypes we assign to people influence how we listen to them. We'd like to believe we're free from these biases, but none of us are.

Different Listening Styles

One person hears with optimism and another with pessimism. I hear the bad news and you hear the good news. If your friend shares a frustrating and difficult situation, you may stop listening because you see it as petty or insignificant. Or you may listen more closely because you view the fact that he is telling you as an act of trust in you.

Not understanding gender differences in listening and conversation creates problems. Women will use more verbal responses like "mm-hmm" to encourage the talker and let them know that they are listening. A man will use this response only when he's agreeing with what a woman is saying. You can see what the outcome could be because of this difference!

A man interprets a woman's listening responses as signs that she agrees with him. But later on, he discovers she wasn't agreeing with him at all. A woman, on the other hand, may feel ignored and disappointed because a man doesn't make the same listening responses she does. She interprets his quietness as not listening.

A man is more likely than a woman to make comments throughout the conversation, but a woman may feel bothered after she's been interrupted or hasn't been given any listening feedback. This is why many women complain, "Men always interrupt" or "They never listen to women."

Inner Struggles

We have difficulty listening when our emotional involvement reaches the point where we are unable to separate ourselves from the other person. What a friend says may cause threatening feelings to surface, or it may activate your own past hurts. As a result, our listening is hindered. We may also experience difficulty in listening if the person has certain expectations of us.

The Habit of Interrupting

When we feel like the other person isn't getting to the point fast enough, we may start asking for information that would be forthcoming anyway. It's easy for our minds to wander, because we think at five times the rate we speak. Even though you process information faster than it can be verbalized, you can choose either to stay in pace with the speaker or let your mind wander. If you're extroverted in your personality you'll struggle with listening. Extroverts tend to interrupt or jump in when there's silence, so they really have to work at overcoming this obstacle.

Mental Overload

The other person is loading you with too much information and you just can't handle it. You feel bombarded with all the details; you don't have enough time to digest them. Your mind feels like a juggler with too many items to juggle, thus it becomes difficult to listen to anything. Relax and catch the basic theme of what's going on.

Bad Timing

Have you made comments such as: "Talk? Now? Well, this isn't the best time," "Just a minute, I need to finish this," or "I'd like to listen, but I'm already late for an appointment"? Choosing the right time to speak can be crucial to the listening process. However, a hurting person will probably come to you at a bad time. You need to decide if you can adapt to listen right then or if you must set up a later time for the discussion.

Physical Exhaustion

Both mental and physical fatigue make it difficult to listen. There are times when you need to let your friend know that right now isn't a good time. But be sure to let him know that you do want to hear what he has to say.

Selective Attention

Another name for this obstacle is filtered listening—screening the information being shared. If you tend to have a negative attitude, you may ignore, distort, or reject positive messages. Often we hear what we want to hear or what fits with our mindset. If we engage in selective listening, we probably engage in selective retention. That means we remember only certain comments and situations.

Listen With Your Whole Body

Concentrate on the person and the message. Give your undivided attention. Turn off the TV when your friend calls to talk. Set aside what you're doing and listen. When you listen with your heart you're helping. A pastor friend told of being called to the home of a man who had just lost his wife. When he came into the house, the man wept and hugged him. Then the pastor went and sat on the couch next to the man. He decided to wait, allowing the husband to take the lead in saying something. He waited for an hour and listened to the sounds of silence. He waited for a second hour to the sounds of silence. Finally the man sighed. My friend broke the silence and asked, "Are you hungry? Would you like me to get us a pizza?"

He said, "Oh yes, that would be great." So the pastor did. He brought it back and they ate. They each said a few words. My friend prayed briefly, patted him on the shoulder, and left. Several weeks later he was surprised to hear that this man had told a number of people he had been helped by the pastor coming over and just spending time with him. Could you have done that? It may be all that your friend needs, just your being present.

Harold Kushner described your ministry:

At some of the darkest moments of my life,
some people I thought of as friends deserted me—some
because they cared about me and it
hurt them to see me in pain; others because
I reminded them of their own vulnerability,
and that was more than they could handle.
But real friends overcame their discomfort and
came to sit with me. If they had no words to make me
feel better, they sat in silence (much better than saying,
"You'll get over it," or "It's not so bad;
others have it worse"), and I loved them for it.
      —Living a Life That Matters[1]

Understanding What
Your Friend Is Experiencing

LIFE IS FULL OF LOSSES. In fact, life is a blending of loss and gain, loss and acquisition.

Any event that destroys our understanding of the meaning of life is felt as a loss. Our beliefs and expectations come under attack.

Losses can be obvious—a stolen car, a burglarized house, or a death or divorce of a loved one. Other losses may not be so obvious. Changing jobs, receiving a less-than-hoped-for amount in a raise, moving, illness (loss of health), a new teacher in mid-semester, the change from an office with windows to one without, a son or daughter going off to school, or the loss of an ideal or lifelong goal—all these are losses.

When the word *loss* is mentioned, death and divorce come to mind. But what about the impact of a diagnosis? "The doctor said it was cancer" or multiple sclerosis or Parkinson's. Or a disability. Where is the ritual in our culture to commemorate the grief of a lifelong disability?

The hardest losses of life are the *threatened* losses. The possibility of them occurring is very present, but there is little that someone can do about them. You've worked for nineteen years at the same company. At twenty years all your benefits will be secure. But then you are informed that due to the sluggish economy and lost contracts, 40 percent of the firm's employees will be terminated at the end of the month, and length of employment is no criteria for being retained. Will you be one of the 40 percent?

There are many other threatened losses in life:

- awaiting the outcome of a biopsy
- a spouse saying, "I'm thinking of divorcing you."
- a business investment that may not come through
- being sued by an angry employee or customer
- being in a foreign country and terrorists threaten to detain everyone as hostages
- a friend telling us he suspects our son has been using drugs.

All of the above are potential losses. They could occur. There is little we can do about them, and we feel the loss before it occurs. We feel helpless.

Types of Losses

The losses we experience in life can be grouped or identified in numerous ways. Several major types of loss could impact any of your friends.

One is the area of *material loss*. It could be the loss of a physical object or even familiar surroundings to which a person has an important attachment.

A *relationship loss* is the ending of opportunities to relate to another person. It involves talking with him, sharing experiences, touching, negotiating, conflicting, and being in the emotional and physical presence of another human being. This loss can come from a move, a divorce, a death, or just growing up.

There are also *intrapsychic losses,* in which our perception or the way we view ourselves undergoes a change. In this, we lose an emotionally important image of ourselves as well as the possibilities of what might have been.

We're all aware of a *functional loss* such as muscular or neurological function in our body. This comes with aging but also all through our life.

Memory losses among the elderly can be devastating.

Role loss impacts all of us. It's a loss of a social role or an accustomed place in some social network. The significance of it depends on how much of our identity was tied to this role. A promotion, demotion, loss of a spouse, change of career, graduation, or retirement all fit here.

During the experience of loss, questions fester beneath the surface but at some point need to be addressed by your friend. You may hear these verbalized:

"Will I recover from this loss? Will I survive?"

"Is it all right to continue with my life without whatever (or whoever) has been lost to me?"

"Can I be happy and fulfilled knowing that the person I've lost is really gone and my life will now be different?"

Adjusting to the Loss of a Family Member

The loss of significant people in our lives is inevitable. Often the loss happens suddenly and traumatically. At other times the loss is expected. Either way, it can be a tremendous crisis, sometimes bringing a significant loss of identity for your friend.

When your friend loses a significant person, he will not only grieve over the person he lost but also over the wishes, needs, hopes, dreams, and unfulfilled expectations he had for the person. And these are important issues you need to help your friend identify. He may also grieve not just for his present loss, but for what he will lose in the future. Perhaps there was something he never had in his relationship with that person, and now he realizes he'll never have it.

When your friend loses a significant person in a sudden, unexpected death, he's at high risk for a pattern of complicated grieving. Sometimes the grief response evolves to a condition known as Post Traumatic Stress Disorder (PTSD). Why does this happen? Consider the cumulative effect of the following factors when anyone's capacity to cope crumbles:

- Your assumptions about control, predictability, and security are lost.
- Your loss makes no sense whatsoever.
- It's difficult to recognize the loss.
- You can't even say good-bye or conclude any unfinished business.
- Your emotional reactions are heightened much more than when a natural death occurs.
- Your symptoms of grief and shock persist, which demoralizes you.
- You may tend to hold yourself responsible more than you normally would.
- You tend to focus on the negative aspects of the relationship with the deceased, rather than having a balanced view.
- You have sudden major secondary losses because of the unexpectedness of the loss.

All of these factors could lead anyone to experience PTSD.[1]

You may be thinking, "I could *never* help a friend in this situation." But you can. The more you know about this, the more you will ease your fear and concern. And in many cases a friend will be the only support that person has.

As your friend recovers from a significant crisis or loss, at times he may be ambushed by grief. There's no other way to describe it. Some call it a "grief spasm." It's an onslaught of grief that hits a person suddenly when he least expects it. He may choke up or cry, his chest may feel constricted, and a wave of sadness may overwhelm him. This is a normal response, but when it happens he needs to stop everything else and deal with his feelings.[2]

One of the tasks of grief is to learn how to function without the other person in his life. Your friend won't have the interactions and validation he was used to experiencing with that person. Talking about this can be helpful. Slowly, over time, the reality of separation will begin to sink in and he will realize, "For now, I exist without this person as a part of my life." This is an important place to arrive at.

Your friend may discover that it will take time to identify all the ways this individual was a part of his life. It's a step-by-step process. The loss of his companionship, support, judgment—all of these are new and separate losses that make up the major loss of his life. Each time he starts to respond to the person who is no longer there, he'll discover again that he or she is gone. There will be many painful reminders.

Whenever someone is gone from anyone's life, roles and skills have to broaden to function without the person. Your friend will need to learn to make up for what he has lost. He changes what he does, takes over new responsibilities, and finds other people to help. There may be some things he doesn't do anymore. Adjustment necessitates not behaving the same way he did when the person was a part of his world.

Steps in the Grief Work Process

Getting on with life involves several steps. Few people are aware of these steps before they experience a major loss.

Some individuals either resist these steps or become "stuck" in their grief. Your presence can help to keep this from happening. Sometimes after people have gone through these stages they are able to sit down and identify what they have experienced. But what a difference it can make in their life if they're aware of the process at the time they're going through it. The awareness doesn't necessarily lessen the pain, but it gives them a map and lets them know they're on track and not going crazy. These steps apply to the more serious kinds of losses.

One of the first things your friend must do is *develop a new relationship* with the person he lost. He has to untie the ties that connected him to this person. The change involves keeping the loved one alive in his memory in a healthy and appropriate manner. Are you comfortable in talking with him about this? (You may want to suggest some reading resources. See list at end of chapter five.)

Formation of a new identity without the other person's presence in his life is another step to take in recovery. As one person said, "That portion of my life is history. I'll never be that way or be that person again."

The Loss of a Spouse

Most couples who marry dream of growing old together. But when a death occurs, there is not only the loss of that dream but all sorts of secondary losses as well. Look at all the roles a spouse fulfills and what is lost when he or she dies:

friend	laundry person
parent	mechanic
handyperson	confidant
protector	encourager
lover	mentor
organizer	motivator
gardener	prayer partner
provider	business partner
companion	source of inspiration or insight
cook	errand person
sports partner	teacher
bill payer	tax preparer
checkbook balancer	counselor

As your friend walks through these steps and does his grief work, the emotional energy he once invested in his spouse is now freed up and reinvested in other people, activities, and hopes that in turn can give emotional satisfaction back to him.

Death ends a loved one's life but not your friend's relationship with that person. How does he develop a new relationship with the person he has lost? This isn't a morbid or odd process. It's a normal response. If people tell your friend that the best way to deal with his loss is to forget the person, very frankly, they're wrong. You don't forget. Someday, way in the future, the emotional memories will become more like historical memories.

We all keep others alive as we reflect upon who they were, their achievements, and their impact upon us and society. Haven't you heard people say, "I wonder what he would think if he were alive today," or "Wouldn't she be surprised to see all of this!"? This is normal.

It may help your friend to be with others who have experienced the same type of loss, for they can assist him in the process of adjusting to his new identity. You may be that person.

The Length of the Mourning Process

How long does it take to recover and complete the mourning process? Much longer than most people believe. The amount of time can vary, depending on many factors.

The average length of mourning is approximately two years for a natural death. In the case of a terminally ill individual, the time following the death could be less, since some of the grieving happened prior to the death.

The unanticipated nature of accidental death can be a major factor in contributing to a grief reaction that lasts for several years. One study indicated that the majority of mourners who experienced the loss of a spouse or child in an automobile accident were still dealing with the death in thoughts, memories, and feelings four to seven years afterward.[3] It could take longer if your friend was involved in the same accident.

You can't tell your friend how long his grief will last, but you can be sure that he'll ask you. Grief has a beginning, a middle, and an end. Many people get stuck in the middle, and most don't understand the dynamics and the duration of grief.

The emotional upheaval associated with bereavement includes a number of common elements: a sense of yearning and searching; a sensitivity to stimuli; feelings of anger, guilt, ambiguity, impatience, and restlessness; and a strong need to test what is real. As you can see from the chart below, these feelings intensify and fade in peaks and valleys.

Intensity Phases of Bereavement[4]

Notice the jagged peaks. The pain and grief actually intensify at three months and then gradually subside, but not steadily. They go up and down. Time after time I've shown this chart in seminars, and people have come up and said, "Why didn't someone warn me about the three-month and one-year anniversary? It would have made it easier to handle. I thought I was going crazy!"

Phases of Bereavement

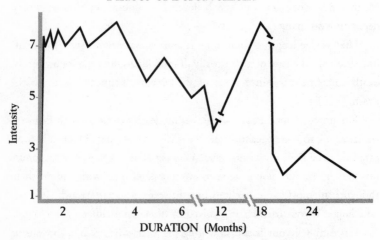

50

There's another phenomenon your friend may experience but not want to share with you or anyone else. It's called the "face in the crowd" syndrome. He's walking along and could swear he saw his loved one at a gathering or heard his loved one's voice. Or he walked into a room on their anniversary and smelled her perfume. This is normal. These experiences can last up to eighteen months after the loss.

The Loss of a Parent

Parental loss is something we all expect, but that doesn't lessen the impact. The first death I experienced with a family member came when I was twenty-two. My father was killed in a traffic accident driving home from work. He was seventy-two. It was a real shock to us. When my mother died in 1993 at the age of ninety-three, it was a loss but not a shock.

When Dad died, there was a sense of missing out on future events, especially since my wife and I discovered the week after the accident that we were going to be parents. Losing the first parent can often be a lingering pain as you constantly witness the effects of this loss on the remaining parent and feel an added responsibility for helping him or her.

When someone loses a parent, he loses a person who for many years has been the most influential person in his life. For most of us, it means losing someone who loved us and cared for us in a way no one else does or ever will again.

When your friend's parent dies he loses his direct link to the past as well as to parts of himself he may have forgotten. Not only that, he will be much more aware of his own mortality. And you'll hear your friend express this. We all feel more vulnerable because our parents aren't there to buffer life's ups and downs. When the second parent dies, it's like the last chapter of a book. For some, it means they can never go home again, psychologically or physically. When you or your friend has to close up a parent's home and sort through what is left, you experience an abundance of secondary losses.

As we grow older, we often become attached to our parents in a new way. It's more of an adult-to-adult or friend-to-friend relationship. I saw this in the closeness of my wife and her mother.

Responses to the death of a parent vary from person to person, depending on the quality of the relationship. For many people, the person they were closest to wasn't a birth parent. It may have been an aunt or uncle or even a surrogate parent. It's important that they face what they are feeling with this loss, experience the fullness of the grief and all the secondary losses, and then move forward without the person.

Not everyone has a good relationship with his or her parents. This can complicate the grief response. In some cases I've seen a person express relief over the death of a parent. For many it's a new chance on life, an opportunity to not have to try to please someone he could never please. Or he may feel relief because his parent's lingering terminal illness made it difficult to care for him or her and was financially draining. This may not have been your experience and this might shock you, especially if you hear some very negative comments.

As your friend grieves the loss of a parent, keep in mind his other family members will grieve differently because of the quality of their relationships with the parent. His siblings, spouse, and children had a different relationship than he did. This could generate conflict unless everyone allows for these differences.

When parents are gone, who takes their place or continues their role? Perhaps they were the peace-keepers for all the children and grandchildren. Who does that now? Perhaps they orchestrated the family get-togethers. Who takes on that role now? Decisions concerning home and property must be made and family heirlooms divided up. The passing of parents will definitely affect their relationship with siblings.

Consideration of some of these changes in advance makes it easier for the surviving family members. These are issues and topics to address at the appropriate time. And if you don't assist your friend at this time, who will?

Understanding a Friend in Crisis

CHAPTER 5

CRISIS — IT'S AN EXPERIENCE that can stop you in your tracks and immobilize you. You're thrown off balance into a state of panic and defeat. It can hit you suddenly or be the last straw in a series of small events.

People will make some of the greatest changes in their lives when they experience a crisis. They're forced to change, since the way they used to solve problems doesn't work anymore. So they're looking for solutions. Your friend may see you as the solution!

What is experienced as a crisis by your friend may not be a crisis to you. You have to see it through her eyes. And to help a friend in crisis you need to understand what constitutes a crisis.

Remember that underlying any crisis is *a loss or series of losses*. Your friend won't be herself; she will be different. She's stunned; her world isn't the same any longer. Her brain is in turmoil. The right side of the brain (the emotional side) has been overwhelmed, which results in an overwhelmed left side (the thinking side). And so in this state a friend reaches out to you.

What is your friend likely to want from you when she talks to you at a time of crisis? People's needs vary. Don't be surprised by the wide range of requests you hear. In many cases, you'll be expected to be a miracle worker. You may be her last hope, and expectations can be excessive, unrealistic, or both. When you can't produce what she wants, don't be surprised if you hear disappointment or anger. Yet you will be able to help in other ways that will meet some of her needs.

What are the different responses you may see from a friend?

You may see someone who wants a strong person to protect and control her. (You can't.)

Another may need someone who will help her maintain contact with reality. (This you can do.)

Someone might feel exceedingly empty and need loving care. (This you can do.)

Some need a helper to be available for a feeling of security. She may call you constantly. (This won't work. Helping is a part-time endeavor, not a full-time job.)

Or you may see the following:

A person with obsessive guilt who is driven to confess. (Only the Lord can handle this.)

An urgent need to talk things out. (You can listen—remember the definition.)

Someone demanding advice on pressing issues: "Tell me what to do." (Be careful. Help her discover the options.)

A person who seeks to sort out her conflicting ideas. (This is possible.)

Your friend may come with *all* of these . . . making *you* feel overwhelmed.

Why Some Adapt Poorly in a Crisis

Of the various friends who seek your help, some will cope quite well with their crises while others cope quite poorly. It is possible to predict which will be which by watching for the following characteristics. People who have them will find their coping skills in a crisis less than adequate.

Overwhelmed. The first characteristic of people who cope poorly is that they are nearly overwhelmed in a crisis. Why? Prior to the crisis they were already struggling emotionally. Now they respond in a way that makes matters worse, but from their perspective they're doing the most efficient thing possible.

Poor physical condition. The second characteristic of those who cope poorly in a crisis is a poor physical condition. They have fewer resources to draw on during a crisis.

Hard time coping. Those who deny reality have a hard time coping with a crisis. Denying reality is their attempt to avoid their pain and anger. They may deny that they're seriously ill, financially ruined, or that their child is on drugs or terminally ill.

Magic of the mouth. This is the tendency to eat, drink, smoke, and talk excessively. When difficulty enters these people's lives, they seem to regress to infantile forms of behavior. Their mouths take over in one way or another. This attempt to not face the real problem can continue after the crisis is over. The person is actually helping to create an additional crisis for herself.

Unrealistic approach to time. People who cope this way crowd the time dimensions of a problem, or they extend the time factors far into the future. In other words, they want the problem to be "fixed" right away, or else they delay and delay. Delaying avoids the discomfort of reality but enlarges the problem. If your friend does this, be prepared for a difficult time in helping.

Excessive guilt. Those who struggle with excessive guilt will have difficulty coping with a crisis. Why? They tend to blame themselves for the difficulty, and by feeling worse immobilize themselves even more.

Blamers. Blamers don't focus on what the problem is but turn to "who caused the problem." Their approach is to find some enemies, either real or imagined, and project the blame upon them.

Excessive dependence or independence. These friends either turn away from offers to help or become clinging vines. The one who clings tends to suffocate you if you're involved in helping her. She'll call you several times a day. Boundaries have little meaning to her. An overly independent friend will shun your offer to help. When the disaster hits, she either continues to deny it or blames others for it.

One other characteristic must be cited that has a bearing upon all the others. A person's theology will affect how he or she copes with a crisis. Our lives are based upon our theology, and yet so many people are frightened by that word. Our belief in God and how we perceive God is a reflection of our theology. Those who believe in the sovereignty and caring nature of God have a better basis from which to approach life.

Phases of a Crisis

As you can see from the chart on the next page, there are four phases in any life-changing event or crisis.

Impact

The impact phase is usually very brief. A person knows immediately that she has been confronted with a major happening. For some people it is like being hit with a two-by-four. This phase involves becoming aware of the crisis and experiencing the effects of it. It lasts from a few hours to a few days, depending upon the event and the person involved. In a severe loss, tears can occur immediately or a few days later. The more severe the crisis or loss, the greater the amount of incapacitation and numbness.

It is possible for the impact phase to linger on and on, as in the case of a divorce proceeding. The person going through it has to make a decision whether to stay and fight the problem through to resolution or run and ignore it. We call this the fight-or-flight pattern. During the impact stage your friend's usual tendency of handling life's problems will probably emerge. If the tendency in the past has been to face problems, she will probably face the problem now. But if her tendency has been to avoid problems, she will probably run from this one.

THE NORMAL CRISIS PATTERN

	Phase I Impact	Phase II Withdrawal/Confusion	Phase III Adjustment	Phase IV Reconstruction/ Reconciliation
Time:	Few Hours to a Few Days	Days to Weeks	Weeks to Months	Months
Response:	Should I stay and face it or withdraw?	Intense emotions. You feel drained. Anger, sadness, fear, anxiety, depression, rage, guilt.	Your positive thoughts begin returning along with all the emotions.	Hope has returned. Self-confidence.
Thoughts:	Numb, disoriented. Insight ability limited. Feelings overwhelm.	Thinking ability limited. Uncertainty and ambiguity.	You're now able to problem solve.	Thinking is clearer.
Direction You Take to Regain Control:	You search for what you lost.	Bargaining/wishful thinking. Detachment.	You begin to look for something new to invest in.	Progress is evident and new attachments are made to something significant.
Searching Behavior:	Often reminiscing	Puzzled, unclear.	You can now stay focused and begin to learn from your experience.	You may want to stop and evaluate where you've been and where you're going.

Emotional Level

Fighting and attempting to take charge again in the midst of crisis seem to be the healthier responses. Running away only prolongs the crisis. And as each of the succeeding phases is dependent upon the adjustments made in the previous one, avoiding reality does not make for good judgment. Pain is prolonged instead of resolved.

Lessened Thinking Capability: Thinking capability is lessened during the impact stage. People are somewhat numb and disoriented. It is even possible for some to feel as though they cannot think or feel at all. The factual information you give your friend may not fully register at this time and may have to be repeated later on. (This is why suggestions, plans you make together, etc., need to be written down in order to be remembered.) You may explain something to her, and she in turn asks a question that indicates she never heard one word. Because she's numb and stunned, she may make unwise decisions. But unfortunately, important decisions may be necessary; postponing them may not be an option. This is where she needs your help. And if you don't have the answers, ask for help yourself.

Searching for the Lost Object: During the impact phase, a person physically and symbolically searches for the lost object. Her thought process is directed toward the loss. It's common for your friend who has lost a loved one in death to take out photographs and other items that remind her of that person. When something that means a great deal to us is lost, we hold on to our emotional attachments longer than we normally would.

Reminiscing about the loss is in proportion to the value of the lost object or person. Your friend needs to be listened to and have her feelings accepted at this point of the crisis. Feeling rejected delays the resolution of the problem. Feelings shouldn't be buried or denied at this point.

Feelings of Guilt: The emotion of guilt frequently accompanies change and crisis. People feel guilty for many reasons, from having failed to having achieved. Many people have difficulty handling success. They wonder if they deserve it, or perhaps they see others who did not succeed and in their empathy for them experience guilt over their own success. Children of parents who divorce sometimes feel guilty, as though they were responsible for the destruction of the marriage. Those who witness accidents or catastrophes often experience guilt. "Why was I spared?" "Why did my young child die and not me? He had so many more years left than I did!" are common reactions.

A friend experiencing guilt has several choices available to her to alleviate the guilt. She can rationalize her way out of the guilt. She can project blame onto others. She can attempt to pay penance and work off the guilt. Or she can apply the forgiveness available where there has been genuine sin and violation of God's principles. God can and does remove true guilt. But there will be other feelings of guilt that have no basis in fact. Forgiveness from God is not usually needed for false guilt. What is needed is help in changing her perspective or self-talk. But this will take time and will probably not be accomplished during the impact phase.

Before we go on to the next stage, let me explain how the use of the previous chart has been helpful for those in crisis. Often this person feels overwhelmed and wonders, "Is my response normal?" On many occasions I have shown people the complete chart, described the various stages, and asked them to indicate where they were on the chart. I usually do this during the second phase, "Withdrawal/Confusion." They respond by first identifying which stage they are in and then saying, "You mean, my response is normal?" By discovering this they feel relieved. Then they're able to see where they will be heading, which further alleviates their anxiety. I carry a laminated copy of the chart with me in my Bible. You may want to do the same.

Withdrawal/Confusion

Intensity in the Emotional Level: One of the key factors in the withdrawal/confusion phase is the intensity in the emotional level. The shock has worn off and those underlying feelings intensify. If you look back at the chart, you will note that each phase becomes progressively longer. This phase, typically the second phase, can last days and even weeks.

Denies Feelings: During this phase, the tendency to deny one's feelings is probably stronger than at any other time. Feelings now can become ugly. Intense anger can occur toward whatever happened, which in some cases brings on guilt for having such feelings. Depression, sadness, fear—these are all part of the denial. Shame can then result, and the pain of all the various feelings can foster a desire to suppress all feelings. This denial leads to emotional, physical, and interpersonal difficulties in time. The best step you can take in helping a friend is to help her identify and put words to her feelings and normalize them, using another chart, the Ball of Grief (see page 64).

Make a copy of this to give to your friend. I use the chart in two ways. One way is that I ask the person to identify which of these feelings she is experiencing. Another way is to ask which of these she *isn't* experiencing. Encourage your friend to take this out each day to identify what she is experiencing.

How do people actually *feel* when confronted by a crisis? What goes on in their emotional spectrum when they find they are unable to adjust to life's major difficulties? You will hear the following:

- A sense of *bewilderment*: "I never felt this way before."
- A sense of *danger*: "I feel so scared—something terrible is going to happen."
- A sense of *confusion*: "I can't think clearly—my mind doesn't seem to work."
- A sense of *impasse*: "I'm stuck—nothing I do seems to help."
- A sense of *desperation*: "I've got to do something, but I don't know what to do."

- A sense of *apathy*: "Nothing can help me—what's the use of trying."
- A sense of *helplessness*: "I can't cope by myself—please help me."
- A sense of *urgency*: "I need help now."
- A sense of *discomfort*: "I feel so miserable and unhappy."

Knowing this emotional spectrum can assist you in relating to the person. You might make statements such as: "Could it be that you just can't think clearly?" "Could it be that you feel stuck, like 'Nothing I do seems to help'?" "Perhaps you feel immobilized, like, 'Why try? Nothing I do seems to help.'"

If your friend's shared feelings begin to shock and alarm you, she'll tend to repress them. But feelings need to be expressed, which means that friends, relatives, or you, along with a social support system, need to be available. A valuable service that you can perform is to develop a strong, ongoing support system that will continue to reach out to your friend in crisis.

Develop a Support System: Over the years I have come in contact with more and more churches that have developed an ongoing ministry for those who have experienced the loss of a loved one. The church arranges for families to minister to the bereaved person in some way (cards, a call, or a meal invitation) each week for a period of two years. This not only involves many from the congregation in ministry but also supports the person over an extended period.

A minister who attended one of my crisis seminars shared that following a funeral or memorial service, he writes the name of the family on his desk calendar every three months for the next two years to remind him to continue to reach out and minister to them over that period of time.

During the withdrawal/confusion phase, your friend *does not* need or benefit from spiritual and psychological insights. Her emotional state, whether it is anger or depression, interferes with the information. We can

BALL OF GRIEF
A TANGLED "BALL" OF EMOTIONS

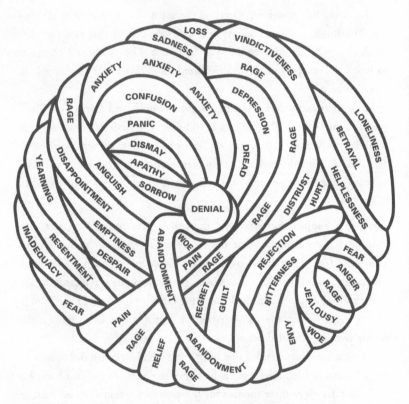

only hope she will be able to draw on what she has already learned, since she will find it difficult to incorporate anything new.

One of the best ways to aid your friend during this phase is to give her some help organizing her life. She needs assistance in arranging appointments, keeping the house in order, and other routine responsibilities. People need this help because they may be suffering from some paralysis of the will.

Above all, when you work with a person in phases one or two, use sustainment responses. These are basic and simple—listening, reassurance, encouragement, and reflection. These approaches will help to lower your friend's anxiety, guilt, and tension, providing emotional support. Your task is to assist in helping her restore some balance into her life.

Self-pity: Another tendency at this phase is self-pity. It's not uncommon for your friend to appear confused. She may approach new people and situations as a type of replacement for what was lost, but then retreat to reminisce. Making a decision during this phase to replace what was lost is not a good idea. The person is not ready, for whatever or whoever was lost has not yet been fully released.

Adjustment

Notice the length of time the third phase, *adjustment,* takes—longer than the others. The emotional responses during this time are hopeful. Some depression may remain or come and go, but positive attitudes have started. Things are looking up. She has just about completed her detachment from what was lost and is now looking for something new to which she can become attached.

Climbing Out: What is occurring in her world begins to take on new importance to her. She has been through the depths of the valley and is now climbing out. What she begins to attach to holds special significance for her. An outsider may not see the same significance and may feel that she is making a mistake by choosing this new job, new home, or new partner. Your friend doesn't need you as a critic, for she is responding from a perspective different from yours.

The one area in which we *do need* to caution the person is selecting a new partner. At this phase it is usually too soon, whether the loss of the spouse is through death or divorce. I encourage people to wait at least a year following their divorce to begin dating. And it's imperative that they complete a divorce recovery program as well. Recovery needs to occur first or they will select a new partner from a position of weakness, bringing the baggage from their previous relationship into the new one.

This may be the time to recommend books or other resources to help your friend recover. Timing is essential and you don't want to force this issue. (Several resources are mentioned at the conclusion of this chapter.)

Hopeful: Remember that, while your friend is becoming hopeful, it is not a consistent hope. She fluctuates and will have down times. She still needs someone to be available. Because insight is returning, she can be objective about what has occurred and can now process new information and suggestions. She can gain new insights spiritually at this point, and her values, goals, and beliefs may be different and have a greater depth.[1] Now is the time to ask questions like, "Where has God been in all of this for you?" "How has this impacted you spiritually?" "What have you learned through all of this that will help you the next time you hit a crisis?"

Reconstruction and Reconciliation

A Spontaneous Expression of Hope: Plans are made out of a new sense of confidence. Doubts and self-pity are gone because your friend has made a logical decision at this point not to engage in them anymore. She takes the initiative for progress, and reattachments are occurring. New people, new places, new activities, new jobs, and new spiritual responses and depths now exist. If there has been anger and blame toward others or if relationships were broken, this is now the time for reconciliation. Forms of reconciliation can include helpful gestures, notes, meals shared together, and doing a helpful act for others.

Reflection of Newness: The final resolution of a crisis is a reflection of the newness of a person. A crisis is an opportunity for your friend to gain new strengths, new perspectives on life, new appreciations, new values, and a new way to approach life. At this time, encourage your friend in the growth you've seen. Continue to pray. The two of you could even talk about how your friend can use what she learned in her crisis to help others.[2]

Resources to Recommend

Loss of a Spouse
Getting to the Other Side of Grief, Susan J. Zonnebelt-Smeenge and Robert C. DeVries (Baker Books, 1998).

Loss of a Child
Safe in the Arms of God, John MacArthur (Thomas Nelson, 2003).

Empty Arms: Hope and Support for Those Who Have Suffered a Miscarriage, Stillbirth, or Tubal Pregnancy, Pamela W. Vredevelt (Multnomah, 1994).

I'll Hold You in Heaven, Jack Hayford (Regal, 1986).

General Helps
A Bend in the Road, David Jeremiah (Thomas Nelson, 2000).

Do Not Lose Heart, Meditations of Encouragement and Comfort, Dave and Jan Dravecky (Zondervan, 1998).

Finding God's Peace in Perilous Times, Tammy Faxel, ed. A book written in response to 9/11 (Tyndale House Publishers, 2002).

Recovering From the Losses of Life, H. Norman Wright (Baker Books, 1991).

What's Happening to My Friend?
It's Called Trauma

THERE'S A NEW WORD IN OUR VOCABULARY. It's *trauma*. Oh, we've heard it before, but since September 11, 2001, it's taken on new significance. Several events in the last fifteen years have made trauma a reality.

First in 1993 at the World Trade Center, next in 1995 in Oklahoma City, then in 1996 during the Olympics, and finally in 2001 at the World Trade Center—again. Americans have now joined much of the rest of the world in facing the reality of terrorism. No longer is this cowardly evil confined to foreign countries. We experienced a twenty-first-century "Day of Infamy"— and life in the United States has been altered radically.

Trauma is the response to any event that shatters our safe world. It's more than a state of crisis. Trauma leaves us feeling unsafe—like our place of refuge has been invaded and forever changed.

Early examples of trauma are recorded in the Bible. Consider Job, who lost his family, farm, and health suddenly and by violent means (Job 1:13–19). David had several close (and no doubt traumatic) encounters with death that involved animals, soldiers, King Saul, and giants (1 Samuel 17:1–52; 18:10–11, 27; 19:8). He also witnessed hand-to-hand combat and thousands of brutal murders. These events affected his personality and altered his immediate family.

The word *trauma* comes from a Greek word that means

"wound." It's a condition characterized by the phrase, "I just can't seem to get over it." This experience is not limited to those who have gone through a war. I've seen it in the father who saw his daughter fatally crushed in an accident years ago and in women who were sexually abused as children; those who have had an abortion have experienced it. I've seen it in the paramedic, the chaplain, and the nurse, and also in the survivor of a robbery, traffic accident, or rape. I heard it in the voice of my neighbor as he described being a witness to an armed robbery in a video store. Trauma touches those subjected to pressure or harassment in the workplace. I also saw it in the face of those impacted by the 2001 terrorist attack in New York City. You may think your friend has experienced a loss, but it could have been trauma, and you may be the one to suggest he see a trauma specialist. But you need to understand what it is in order to help.

What's Trauma Like?

What we used to see as a safe world is no longer safe. What we used to see as a predictable world is no longer predictable. Most people overestimate the likelihood that life is going to be relatively free from major crises or traumas. Most underestimate the possibility of negative events happening to them. Perhaps that's why we're so devastated and our core beliefs shaken when they do. What beliefs do you and your friend hold about life? What will happen to those beliefs if either of you experiences trauma? It's important to ask yourself these questions *before* trauma enters your life or anyone else's.

Perhaps you're asking the question that most people ask: "How widespread are traumatic events in our country? How many people are exposed to traumatic events, such as natural and technological disasters, accidents, crime, abuse, or war?"

We used to say 75 percent of the general population in our country has been exposed to some event that meets the criteria for trauma. Now it's even higher. The good news is that only about 25 percent of those exposed to such events become *traumatized*.[1] But those who are traumatized need help as soon as possible.

Physical trauma affects a person in two ways. Obviously, some part of the body is impacted with such a powerful force that the body's natural protection, such as skin or bones, can't prevent the injury, and the body's normal, natural healing capabilities can't mend the injury without some assistance.

Perhaps not as obvious is the emotional wounding caused by trauma. Our psyche can be so assaulted that our beliefs about ourselves, our life, our will to grow, our spirit, our dignity, and our sense of security are damaged. People can experience this to some degree in a crisis and still bounce back. In trauma they have difficulty bouncing back because they feel derealization (*Is this really happening?*) and depersonalization (*I don't know what I really stand for anymore*).

Trauma's Effect on the Brain

As the result of trauma, something happens in our brain that affects the way we process information. It affects how we interpret and store the event we experienced. In effect, it overrides our alarm system. Trauma has the power to disrupt how we process incoming information. When we can't handle the stress, we activate our survival techniques.[2]

Most of us aren't aware of what happens to our brain. There's an alarm portion of the brain that controls our behavior. When we've been traumatized, this alarm system becomes hypersensitive. It overreacts to normal stimuli. For example, it sees a large person and feels *He's going to hurt me. Oh no!*

But another part of the brain is analytical and calms down the emotional part of the brain—it analyzes things and puts things into perspective. *No, a large person isn't necessarily going to hurt me.*

In trauma it's as though the left side (the cognitive) and the right side (the emotional) are disconnected from one another. As one man said, "I feel like my brain was disrupted and one part is transmitting the AM and the other the FM. Sometimes there are holes in my memory like a slice was taken out. Other times I can't get those intrusive unwanted memories to stop. I want them evicted! I can't remember what I want to remember and I can't forget what I want erased." This struggle is familiar to those who undergo trauma.[3]

Susceptibility to Trauma

Are some people more susceptible to being traumatized than others? If your friend is "emotionally healthy," if he came from a "healthy home," if he's a "strong Christian," is he immune to this disorder? No. Neither are you. We're all susceptible to trauma.

If you or a friend becomes traumatized, it's *not* because of a defect in either of you. Your reactions are normal in response to an abnormal event. Yes, we do vary in our responses and our capacity for endurance. Some people have better coping skills than others. Those who have a strong faith in Jesus Christ and an accurate understanding of life through the Scriptures have more resources to help them cope. But for all of us there may come a point in time when our defenses are overrun.[4]

There's one last factor to consider. Those who are involved in natural catastrophes seem to experience shorter and less intense post-traumatic stress disorder (PTSD) than those involved in man-made disasters. If a natural disaster can be seen as an act of nature or God—*that's just life*—the survivors don't lose as much trust in others as those involved in man-made disasters. Another word for man-made is *atrocity*. That's why Oklahoma City, Columbine, and New York City have impacted us so much.[5]

What experiences might create traumas in our lives? There are so many events.

Trauma can occur in the survivors of a refugee or concentration camp. Many people have become traumatized through sexual or physical assault. For some children, trauma is not Oklahoma City—it's going home at night.

Children who were physically mistreated by excessive beatings, spankings, confinement, or deprivation of food or medical care can be seriously affected for life.

We can be traumatized by witnessing a death or serious injury in a car accident; by seeing a victim of a violent crime beaten, raped, or killed; by being exposed to an uprising, riot, or war. Children, who have even less capability than adults to handle significant events in their lives, can be more easily damaged.

Many of the conditions mentioned so far pertain to being a witness. When it happens to you, it's even worse. Any situation in which you feel that you or another family member could be killed or hurt gives you cause to experience trauma.

Those involved in the helping profession are open to trauma if they've been involved in just one of the following conditions:

- witnessed death and injury
- experienced a threat to their own safety and life
- made life-and-death decisions
- worked in high-stress conditions

This doesn't mean that PTSD or being traumatized is necessarily a result, but the event has potential to lead to it.[6]

Keep in mind that sometimes what is traumatic to one person may not be to another. We can't always choose who comes to us for help, but we *can* choose to be there for them—to be present, to listen, and to pray. For many, this will do wonders.

What Does Trauma Do?

CHAPTER 7

TRAUMA HAS MANY EFFECTS. It shatters our beliefs and assumptions about life, challenges our belief that we have the ability to handle life, and tears apart our belief that the world is a just and orderly place to live. That's quite dramatic, isn't it? Whether it's your friend or you, here is what to expect:

Trauma leads to silence: *I don't have the words to describe it.*

Trauma leads to isolation: *No one seems to understand or enters into the experience I had.*

Trauma leads to feelings of hopelessness: *There was no way to stop what happened or the memories of what happened.*[1]

Our level of optimism begins to crumble.

We all want a reason for what happens to us. We want to know *why* so that we can once again have a sense of order and predictability about life. But in trauma we end up with unanswered questions. And your friend will have a number of them.

She might say, "I always thought right would prevail as well as justice. What happened seems so unfair!" What do we do when we expect the good guys to always win and the bad guys to always lose, and it doesn't turn out that way?

Job said it well: "Behold, I cry out of wrong, but I am not heard: I cry aloud, but there is no judgment" (Job 19:7 KJV).

We all want answers, expect answers, plead for answers, but sometimes heaven remains silent. That's when our faith undergoes a crisis in addition to whatever else is impacting us.

Trauma also affects how your friend sees herself—her self-identity. She may see herself as a rational, strong, take-charge, in-control person . . . before the event. A trauma changes all that.

Re-experiencing Trauma

At times your friend may *re-experience the trauma.* Thoughts, pictures, dreams, nightmares, or even flashbacks of what happened may occur. Sometimes it may slip into her mind like a video stuck on continuous replay. This sensitivity can become so extreme that an event can trigger a flashback and make her feel and act as if she were experiencing the original trauma all over again. This is a normal response.

The anniversary of the event may serve as a trigger or reminder. As the date draws near, the intensity of the actual trauma can build. Holidays and other family events can create strong emotional responses as well. It's possible for a traumatized person to be set off by something she sees, hears, smells, or tastes. In the case of abuse, a confrontation with the abuser may bring back emotional or physical reactions associated with the abuse. It helps to forewarn your friend about such a possibility.

Even the system that is designed to help a victim can cause her to relive the painful event. It could be the court system or sentencing process, the police, or the mental health system. You may need to accompany your friend to one of these encounters. Certainly the media doesn't help in their graphic coverage of the worst incidents in life, nor do the movies in their extensive portrayals of violence. These portrayals can also bring back the memories of a traumatized person's victimization.[2] Encourage your friend to avoid certain programs—especially the news at bedtime.

In a flashback it's as though the person leaves the present and travels back in time to the original event. She sees it, hears it, and smells it. Sometimes a person begins to react as if she were there. A flashback is like a cry of something that needs to come out and does so in the only way it knows how. When survivors can talk about the trauma, write about it, and bring it to God in an honest and real way through worship, there isn't as great a need for this memory to be so intrusive in nightmares, images, or flashbacks. And at first your job may be for you to not only accompany your friend to the worship service but also let others know what to expect and how to respond.

Another way that someone re-experiences trauma is through *painful and angry feelings* that seem to come out of nowhere. These feelings occur because they were repressed at an earlier time. Now the emotions are simply crying out for release. Listen to your friend and don't take it personally.

Or your friend may re-experience trauma through *numbing and avoidance.* It's painful to re-experience trauma. For some, it's agonizing. She wants it to go away and disappear forever, but it doesn't. So her body and her mind take over to protect against the pain. This is done by emotional numbing. It can create a diminished interest in all areas of life. She may feel detached from others around her—even the ones she loves the most. Often there is no emotional expression because she's shut everything down.[3]

When your friend re-experiences trauma, sometimes she feels some of the emotion she didn't experience at the time of the event because of the numbing that took place. Now when feelings of rage, anger, guilt, anxiety, fear, or sadness emerge she'll wonder, *Where did these come from? They hurt! I don't want them!* She will shut down again so she won't feel as if she's going through a series of out-of-control mood swings. She may begin to avoid situations she thinks may trigger this condition. If she was robbed in a restaurant, she may avoid restaurants. I've seen fire fighters, police officers, and medical personnel seek another line of work after they've been traumatized.

There's something else you can expect to see in a traumatized friend. She's on alert in a state usually referred to as *hyperalertness* or *hyperarousal.* The strong emotions we experience—fear, anxiety, anger—affect the traumatized person's body, particularly her adrenaline output.

During a traumatic event, the heart begins to race, breathing is difficult, and muscles tighten. Some, in an attempt to make sense of what is happening to them, mislabel their bodily responses. They may say, "I'm going crazy," "I'm going to collapse," "I'm going to have a heart attack," or "I'm dying." Some never correct the way they label these bodily responses. So any time their heart pounds or it's hard to breathe, they misinterpret what's happening and end up with a panic attack.[4] This could be frightening to you if you've never seen a panic attack.

For some victims of trauma, emotions—such as fear—rage out of control. I've worked with many people who were paralyzed by fear. You may have a friend like this. Sometimes she's afraid to make a decision, risk another's disapproval, or take a stand. She may be afraid that others don't like her. And even worse, she's afraid to break out of this pattern she is trapped in.

This discussion on trauma is basic and oversimplified. It's informational. But you need information to understand what your friend is experiencing. The information is meant to alert you to the fact that trauma exists and is perhaps closer to you than you realize. If you identify yourself as one of those experiencing any degree of PTSD, or you know someone who fits the characteristics, remember this:

1. *Being traumatized is not incurable*; recovery is possible, but it is a slow process. Your friend needs to hear this.
2. *Your friend will need to work with a professional,* someone who is equipped to assist those experiencing trauma. This could be a highly trained minister, chaplain, or therapist.
3. *Control can come through understanding.* The more you learn about trauma for yourself or for others, the more you and the other person will feel in control of life.

The Other Side of Trauma

Keep in mind that there is another side to trauma. The current research on those who have been traumatized indicates the majority of victims say they *eventually benefited* from the trauma in some way. And these are people who experienced as much pain as those who have never fully recovered. How did they benefit? There was a change of values, a greater appreciation for life, a deepening of spiritual beliefs, a feeling of greater strength, and an ability to build stronger relationships.

"The most important element in recovering is to remain connected to other people."[5] Your friend needs other people to walk with her at this time of life more than any other.

One of the best steps for your friend to take is to stop seeing herself as a person who is diseased or deficient. Your friend is not abnormal because of her trauma symptoms; it is the *event* she experienced that was abnormal. The event was so out of the ordinary that it overwhelmed her, as it would anyone—including you.[6]

Three Stages of Recovery

How will your friend recover? She will need to go through the *thinking stage,* the *emotional stage,* and the *mastery stage.* The *thinking stage* involves fully facing her trauma, remembering it, and even reconstructing it mentally. This isn't a matter of dwelling in the past but of taking fragmented and disconnected memories and pulling them together so that your friend can make sense of the present. Sometimes this stage involves talking with others (like you), re-creating the scene, or reading any written accounts of it. When this is accomplished she will be able to view what happened from a new perspective—an objective view rather than a judgmental view.[7]

In the thinking stage she needs to look at what happened to her as a detached observer (even though it may be difficult) rather than as an emotionally involved participant. If she's able to work through this stage, she will acquire a new assessment of what her real choices were during the traumatic experience. She'll have a better understanding of how the event has impacted the totality of her life and will be able to reduce the self-blame that most experience. Finally, she'll gain a clearer understanding of who or what she may be angry at.[8]

The thinking stage deals with the mental area, but healing and recovery must also involve the *emotional* level. This second stage will necessitate dealing with any of the feelings she may have repressed because of the trauma. Feelings hurt. Those emotions (anger, anxiety, grief, fear, sadness, etc.) must be expressed on the gut level. This isn't easy; many people have a fear of feeling worse and losing control. Your friend doesn't have to act on the feelings, nor will they take over her life. But she does need to face them.[9] How can you help? If your friend shows signs of anger, have her draw a picture of her anger, whisper to it in as loud a voice as possible, give it other names, write a letter to her anger, or have her anger write one back to her. The possibilities are endless.

The final stage is the *mastery stage*. This is when your friend finds new meaning through what she's experienced, and her perspective becomes that of a survivor rather than a victim. Who has greatest potential to become a survivor? A person who has a relationship with Jesus Christ and a biblical worldview.

Mastering the trauma involves making her own decisions instead of allowing experiences, memories, or other people to make decisions for her. This is a time of growth, change, and new direction in her life. What anyone learns because of a trauma probably could not have been learned any other way. Look at what Scripture says about this:

> *Blessed be the God and Father of our Lord Jesus Christ, the Father of mercies and God of all comfort, who comforts us in all our affliction so that we may be able to comfort those who are in any affliction with the comfort with which we ourselves are comforted by God. For just as the sufferings of Christ are ours in abundance, so also our comfort is abundant through*

Christ. But if we are afflicted, it is for your comfort and salva-
tion; or if we are comforted, it is for your comfort, which is
effective in the patient enduring of the same sufferings which
we also suffer. (2 Corinthians 1:3–6 NASB)

How can a person tell if she's progressing and moving ahead? Symptoms become less frequent and the struggle with fear less intense. One of the fears that is so disheartening is the fear of going crazy or insane.

There will be times when the only way to get rid of anger and feelings of revenge is to face the fact that nothing can be done to change what happened or prevent a similar occurrence in the future. Then the next step is to begin to give up a portion of her anger or resentment each day. It's like saying, "All right, today I'm giving up 5 percent of my anger and tomorrow another 5 percent."

As your friend moves through her journey to recovery, the rigidity that helped her cope will diminish. She'll gradually discover the value of flexibility and spontaneity to the degree that she's comfortable with it, based on her unique personality.

One of the delights of recovery is developing a new appreciation of life. Your friend will begin to see what she wasn't seeing before, to hear what she couldn't hear before, to taste what was tasteless before.

Some people rediscover their sense of humor and all its healing properties.

They'll discover a new and deeper sense of empathy for the wounded around them. A trauma survivor can actually become a wounded healer and have a greater compassion for others. The verse that says "Weep with those who weep" takes on a new meaning (Romans 12:15 NASB).[10]

When your friend has experienced trauma, sometimes that's all she remembers. What would happen if she were able to leapfrog over that event back to what her life was like before the trauma? We call this "looking at your life as it was." What was her life like? What did she do each day? You could assist her in answering the following questions to help recapture time before the trauma. The questions include:

What was your biggest struggle then?
What fulfilled you?
What did you enjoy the most?
What did you look like then? (It helps to be very specific about this. Sometimes pictures and videos help the process.)
Who were your friends?
What did you like and not like about yourself?
What did you believe about God then?
What were your Christian practices, such as prayer?
What were your goals or dreams for yourself then?
What are your goals or dreams for yourself now?
What would you like to be different now?

As your friend looks at what she wrote, help her decide what is different now. What alternatives can she think of to make her life more the way she wants it to be?

Overcoming trauma is a process—a journey. But we don't travel the journey alone; the Lord is with us.

The Spirit of the Sovereign Lord is on me, because the Lord has anointed me to preach good news to the poor. He has sent me to bind up the brokenhearted, to proclaim freedom for the captives and release from darkness for the prisoners. (Isaiah 61:1)

Remember—you *can* help. Be there for your friend. Listen with your heart, reach out with the hands of Jesus, and pray.[11]

Helping a Friend in a Crisis or Trauma

CHAPTER 8

WHEN A FRIEND CALLS AND NEEDS your help there is a set way to respond. Remember that you are helping as a compassionate friend. Keeping this in mind will encourage you to pray more and be dependent on the leading of the Holy Spirit for listening, words, and direction. Some of the same suggestions apply whether your friend has experienced a crisis or a trauma.

As you are gathering information from his story and answers to your questions, you're seeking to discover the following: (1) Which issues in your friend's life need to be attended to immediately? and (2) Which issues can be postponed until later? Help him make this determination, because so often people in crisis are not aware of what can wait and what must be handled at once. Sometimes it's as simple as getting him some food and rest. As you work more in crisis situations, you will discover that you seldom have to conduct a question-by-question approach to derive critical information. Your friend will volunteer most of it. But as you discuss the situation with him, *be sure to keep the questions in this chapter in mind.*[1]

Be aware of your friend's level of alertness and communication capabilities. Attempt to identify the cause of the crisis: "Tell me what has happened to make you so upset." *Telling his story as he experienced it is foundational.* Don't start with feelings, which is what many people are prone to do. "Tell me how you're feeling" is *not* the starting point.

Those in a crisis sometimes have difficulty stating clearly what they want to say. When this occurs, you'll need to be extremely patient. Any verbal or nonverbal indication of impatience, discomfort, or urging your friend to hurry is counterproductive. Allow for pauses and remain calm. Remember that especially during the impact phase of the crisis there is a stage of confusion and disorientation; the mental processes are not functioning as they normally would. Some of the pain is so extreme that the words will not come easily.

Sometimes what you hear will not sound rational because it isn't. Helping a devastated friend will tap your energy and push your ability to be flexible to the wall. It's common and normal for you to think *Will this ever end?* or *I don't know how much more of this I can take.*

Help for You, the Caregiver

Before becoming significantly involved in helping others, you need to be aware of a problem that none of us are immune to. It has different names, such as *compassion fatigue, helper shutdown,* or *helper burnout,* and it can happen to doctors, nurses, counselors, rescue workers, or anyone involved in helping others. It seems to be a case of emotional contagion— you end up catching the disorder of the person or people you are helping. When you minister to a friend, he may leave feeling better, but you're stressed because you've absorbed his problems emotionally as well as mentally.

This can happen for several reasons. It can be an overload if you're helping a number of hurting individuals at the same time. The desire to help others is good, but you need to realize that not everyone will be helped and there are some who aren't willing to take steps to change. You may end up with what we call "mission failure" or "I didn't help them enough." We need to remember that the one bringing the changes is the Lord; we have to relinquish others to His care. Your value in helping others is to be there for them and follow the helpful guidelines. Don't evaluate your effectiveness on how well they respond.

What will especially impact you is helping children who have experienced trauma. This affects even the most experienced professional helper.

To guard against helper burnout, make sure you maintain a balance in your life. You need to have times just for tending to and nurturing yourself through the Word, healthy friendships, exercise, recreation, devotional reading, laughter, and allowing others to care for you.

Sometimes you discover that helping certain friends is just too draining. You'll feel empty after every encounter and your friend may need assistance from someone other than you. Be aware of your thoughts. If you're constantly thinking about your friend's problems and you don't relinquish his issues to the Lord, you could end up in difficulty.

Two resources you may want to read and recommend to those you help are *Making Peace With Your Past*[2] and *Winning Over Your Emotions*.[3]

Responding to a Friend in Crisis

As you listen to your friend, notice if he's expressing any important themes. You might notice that he is repeating statements or speaking with great intensity. These are clues to the person's point of distress.

After your friend has described what's happened, you could ask, "What thoughts went through your mind at this time?" Since his thoughts are in such disarray right now, you're trying to help him reduce the clutter and cobwebs. As your friend begins to think a bit more clearly (and this will come and go), he will feel a bit more in control. But remember that he may not remember all of what happened, and this might bother him. You can reassure him that this is normal for what he's been through.

Eventually ask, "What was your reaction or response to this?" If you're talking with a man, use the words *response* and *reaction*, since many men don't relate to the word *feelings*.

On occasion you may need to channel the direction of the conversation. Some crisis situations need *immediate* action rather than waiting until tomorrow or next week. You can reinforce statements that are related to the crisis and avoid responding to unrelated topics, such as rambling statements that deal with the past or peripheral events. This process of focusing helps filter out any material that is irrelevant to the crisis. Often the person himself cannot make this distinction. A gentle supportive tone is very important.

If you're confused by what is said, don't hesitate to ask for clarification. When he's able to express the issues fairly clearly, help him to explore the alternatives available to deal with the situation. Ask questions such as: "What else might be done at this time?" Discover what other support systems your friend has if you don't know—spouse, parents, friends, or fellow workers.

Anyone in a crisis will interpret his environment as something that's difficult to manage. He sees confusion, perhaps even chaos. Try to determine if you might be able to bring a greater sense of order to his environment. If you can assist in bringing a sense of calm, stability, and relief, believe me, this will be appreciated! Perhaps your friend needs to stay at a different location for a while. He may need some space and quiet, or even need to be away from others who are attempting to help but actually add to the confusion by their inappropriate attempts.

As the person talks with you, assess what he's telling you and compare it to the problem as you see it. Remember, often a crisis is triggered by the person's *perception* of what has occurred. There may be times when you feel your friend is overreacting, but remember that what he is reacting to might not be the main problem. Some people fall apart over an insignificant occurrence that's really only a trigger mechanism. There may be a blocked or delayed response to another crucial problem.

The Caregiver's Role

An often asked question is, "How do I know how much action to take?" A rule of thumb is this: Only if circumstances severely limit your friend's ability to function do you take extensive action. And when you do, you want to move him to an independent role as soon as possible.

If the crisis is likely to result in danger to your friend or others, if he's emotionally overwhelmed and has no capability to function or take care of himself, if he's on drugs or alcohol, or if he's injured, *then* you would take a more *directive role.*

When your friend isn't a danger to others or himself, when he's capable of making phone calls, running errands, driving, and caring for himself or others, your role is *facilitative.* The two of you may make the plans together, but your friend needs to carry out the plan. You may even want to work out a contract with him, detailing how the plans are to be carried out.

Whether you are taking directive action or a facilitative role, *listening* and *encouraging* are primary tools. Often I show the person I'm helping the crisis sequence chart described in chapter 5; this helps to relieve pressure.

Before you take action, ask yourself questions such as:

> *"Is this something my friend could do for himself?"*
> *"What will this accomplish in the long run?"*
> *"How long will I need to be involved in this way?"*
> *"Are there any risks in doing this? If so, what are they?"*
> *"How could my friend be helped in a different manner?"*

Your friend's feeling of helplessness is strong during a crisis; you can counter this helpless feeling by encouraging him to create alternatives and take action. This will also help him operate from a position of strength rather than weakness.

Coach him to consider the possibility that there are other alternatives. Some statements can be structured in a tentative, open-ended way: "Let's consider this possibility. What if you were to . . ." "What might happen if you would . . ." "Let's think of a person you feel is a real problem solver. What might that person do?" Be sure to help him anticipate any obstacles to implementing the plan. We cannot assume that he will follow through without first considering the obstacles.[4]

One way you can assist is by helping your friend avert a catastrophe and move toward a state of balance. If he's just lost his job he could, with your help, make a list of his qualifications, abilities, and job experiences. Just the simple task of completing some action can provide a sense of relief.

Since anyone in crisis or trauma feels hopeless, it's important to *foster hope and positive expectations*. Don't give false promises, but encourage him to solve his problems. Your belief in your friend's capabilities will be important. This is a time when he needs to borrow your hope and faith until his own returns.

The problem-solving approach, rather than giving false reassurances, is a positive step. On occasion it's helpful to ask about past crises and upsets to discover how he handled them. If you are familiar with some of these, you could refer to his handling of them. This helps him see that he has been able to work through past problems, which can instill hope for the current problem. Help your friend set goals for the future if he is at that phase of the crisis sequence.

As his anxiety level drops, he'll see the situation in a more objective manner. When this occurs, he can reflect on what has happened and what is now occurring. Don't be surprised when laughter occurs. As there's a time to weep, there's also a time to laugh. We all look to humor to help us take a break from the heaviness of our loss or other tragedy.

You can help your friend restore balance in several important ways.

First, look at the information he's giving you about the situation. Does he see the complete picture or only selected aspects? Does he have all the facts? Is he distorting the situation because of his emotions or his own biases? Does he understand that certain responses and feelings are normal during a time of crisis?

Asking pertinent questions and prodding for informational answers can help. (1) You can help to fill in some of his informational gaps, and (2) his fears and concerns can be diminished as he receives accurate information. Both steps help to restore equilibrium.

How well does your friend grasp the choice of action open to him in light of the recent changes in his life (such as the loss of a job or a spouse)? What options are open to him (such as caring for the children if a spouse has died or left)? Anyone in this situation needs help considering the choices and the consequences of decisions both to himself and others who may be involved.

Providing Support

What else can you do? You can provide support. One of the reasons a problem develops into a crisis is the lack of an adequate social support system. Intervention in a crisis involves giving support, and initially *you* may be the only one giving it. Just being available to talk by phone is a source of support.

The knowledge that you are praying for your friend each day and are available to pray with him over the phone is a source of support. Don't be surprised by a number of "urgent" calls during the early steps of a crisis. These need to be returned promptly and often. Their purpose is to gain support just through simple contact with you.

It's important to return calls promptly, but that's not the same as immediately. If you drop everything you're doing to call back, a dependency relationship could be encouraged and your day will end up in chaos.

If you let a half hour go by, your friend will have the opportunity to do some thinking on his own. He may calm down, and by the time you talk to him, the problem or issue will no longer be critical. This is important, because it takes you out of the magical miracle-worker role.

The best way of supporting your friend is to expand his support system as soon as possible. This reduces demands on you. It helps him through the immediate crisis, and it can help to prevent a crisis in the future.

Try to determine what type of support system your friend has. Does he have any relatives or friends in the area? Are they functional, or will they drag your friend down? These need to be people who replenish rather than deplete. Whom has he told about his difficulty? Learn about the helping agencies—such as those that provide financial or housing support or a suicide prevention center—in your area so you can direct him toward such help when needed. Neighbors and friends can provide baby-sitting or transportation. People from the church can provide cooked meals over a period of time. Try to determine whom he can draw on and what they can do to reduce the pressures upon him during his crisis. This is a very practical way of helping.

Be sure you give some specific guidance to the support people. They're not to give a lot of verbal advice, which may be well intended but unnecessary. Sometimes you will need to give some direct guidance, even though it seems uncomfortable. But whoever said helping a friend is easy? It costs in time and energy. But it's worth it.

Recommended Reading

When Your World Falls Apart: Life Lessons From a Ground Zero Chaplain, Mike MacIntosh (Victor Books, 2002).

Will My Life Ever Be the Same? H. Norman Wright (Harvest House, 2002).

Help! My Friend Is Depressed

CHAPTER 9

I'M NOT SURE WHAT TO DO for this friend. Every time she calls she's either depressed or worried sick. I know she's been through a lot recently and I wish she'd get some help. I'm not sure what to say or do. I don't want to make the problem worse." Many of us find ourselves in this quandary at some time. You may be the first link in helping your friend find the help she needs.

Keep in mind that depression is a very normal response to losses and trauma.

If your friend is depressed, she desperately needs someone to help her. But she may not be able to communicate to you what she is experiencing. If you haven't felt hopeless and helpless yourself, it may not be easy for you to understand what she is going through.

Picture the depressed person down in a deep pit. The pit is dark, cold, and very isolated; it is frighteningly lonely. On all sides there are only rocky walls; there are no handholds or solid footholds that would provide a way to climb up and out. The person in the pit is completely helpless and easily becomes resigned to days of darkness and despair. There seems to be no way of escape.

This is how your friend feels when she has sunk to the depths of depression. She feels overwhelmed and imprisoned by nagging but deadly feelings of worthlessness, fear, and self-blame.

Helping Those Who Hurt

Concerned friends or family members stand above on the edge of the pit, yearning to help. Even so, it's very hard to call for help from the paralyzing helplessness of depression. Sometimes it's difficult to admit to others that you're even down there.[1]

As you offer help to your depressed friend, pray for understanding and patience. You'll need an abundance of both. Your offer to help may be rejected at first, and it could be some time before it is accepted. You can't just go down into the pit, grab her, and hoist her to the top. You'd like to, but it doesn't work that way. Your friend must be willing to trust God and other people. She must decide to begin to climb out of the pit herself. Your encouragement will be like a ladder placed inside the pit; it may give her the motivation and hope to begin the climb.

This is also a time to help her grasp the hope found in the Word of God.

Do you not know? Have you not heard?
The Everlasting God, the Lord, the Creator of the ends of the
*   earth*
Does not become weary or tired.
His understanding is inscrutable.
He gives strength to the weary,
And to him who lacks might He increases power.
Though youths grow weary and tired,
And vigorous young men stumble badly,
Yet those who wait for the Lord
Will gain new strength;
They will mount up with wings like eagles,
They will run and not get tired,
They will walk and not become weary. (Isaiah 40:28–31 NASB)

If you're around a depressed person you will have to protect two people—you and her. Why? Because the depression will affect both of you. You're dealing with someone who is very sensitive, and you must exhibit a certain sensitivity toward her. But you may feel angry and irritated at the way she is acting, which in turn can make you feel guilty for feeling that way. Because of your anger you may respond in ways that make you even angrier, especially at yourself. Your friend will sense this and feel even worse because she feels that she is a burden on you. In time you may feel drained.

If you're depressed yourself, you should not attempt to help someone else with her depression or you'll find yourself feeling overwhelmed. Your relationship could become strained too.

What can you say to a friend or relative who is going through depression? Simply, "I care for you and I am available. I want to help you and be with you." Put your arm around the person and hold his or her hand. There is healing in our physical touch. A touch on the shoulder, a pat on the back, or holding the arm all convey acceptance and the feeling, "I am with you." Be honest and tell the person, "I don't understand all that you are going through, but I am trying to understand. I will be here to help you."

Practical Guidelines to Follow

Most people don't know what to do for a depressed person. Here are some practical guidelines to follow. How closely you follow these will depend upon the intensity and duration of the person's depression. If she is depressed for only a few hours or a day or two, or if she is feeling down but is functioning, not all the suggestions apply. But if the depression has lasted for weeks or months and she is dragging, not functioning, not eating, and/or not sleeping, apply the appropriate measures.

1. The first step toward helping is to *understand the causes and*

symptoms of depression. If your friend is so depressed that she just stares, ignores greetings, or turns away from you, remember that she doesn't want to act that way. In depression, a person loses the ability to govern her thinking and her emotions.

2. *Watch out for suicide.* Any hint, statement, or allusion to suicide should be talked about. I know it's difficult to accept that your friend would ever consider this, but it does happen. It helps the depressed person to bring it out into the open and talk about it. Then she knows that other people are aware and can be called upon for help and support.

3. *Encourage your depressed friend to see a doctor.* Your family physician may be able to help or recommend someone who can. The time factor is very important. Don't let depression go on and on. Even if your friend keeps putting you off and refusing to go, make the arrangements, guide her firmly into the car, and go!

4. To help you *identify the extent of your friend's depression,* use the diagram below. Show your friend the diagram and ask her to indicate where she is at this moment with her depression:

0 . . . . 5 10

Not depressed at all	A few clouds	It's getting overcast	The sky is darker	Heavy depression

If you are helping your friend over a period of time, you could have her evaluate her depression each month and note her progress.

5. *Give your friend your full support.* Her entire family ought to be made aware of the situation and given instructions as to their responses. Confrontations with the depressed person should be suspended until she achieves greater stability. Tell the family not to attack her, bring up her failures, or come down hard on her.

6. *Don't avoid a depressed friend.* This further isolates her and could make her worse. Some might avoid her because they experience guilt over

her depression, thinking that they may be the cause. Remember that one person may contribute to another's problem from time to time, but no one is responsible for another person's unhappiness.

7. *Understand that a depressed friend really does hurt.* Don't suggest that she doesn't really feel bad or that she is just trying to get your sympathy. Don't tell her that all she has to do is "just pray about it and read the Word more" and that will solve everything. Often a depressed person chooses portions of the Scripture that reinforce her feelings of loss and unworthiness. Any Scriptures given to a depressed person must be selected with care.

8. *Empathize, rather than sympathize,* with your friend. Sympathy can only reinforce the feelings of hopelessness. Sympathizing with her may make her feel more helpless and lower her already low self-esteem.

Remember that any depressed person's complaints are expressions of emotional pain. Don't get embroiled in a battle over the content of the statement. Stick with her feelings. Here are some specific guidelines:

- "I'm all alone."
  Don't say: "No you're not! I'm sitting here with you right now. Doesn't my friendship mean anything?"
  Do say: "I know that you're feeling alone right now. Is there anything I can do to help? Together we'll get through this lonely feeling."
- "Why bother? Life isn't worth living. There's no point in going on."
  Don't say: "How can you think that? You have two beautiful children and a great job. You have everything to live for."
  Do say: "I know it feels that way to you right now, but I want you to know that you matter to many. You will get through this hopeless feeling."
- "I'm dragging everyone else down with me."
  Don't say: "No you're not. You see? I'm fine. I had a good day today.

And besides, I'm doing everything in the world to help you."

Do say: "I know it feels that way right now. And yes, at times it is difficult for others, but everyone will get though this burdened feeling together."

- "What would it be like if I weren't here anymore?"

  Don't say: "Don't talk crazy! What's wrong with you?"

  Do say: "There are many, including me, who would miss you terribly. You're important to us. We'll all help and get through this together."

- "I'm expendable."

  Don't say: "If you felt better about yourself, you wouldn't say stupid things like that."

  Do say: "I know you're feeling worthless right now, but we'll get through this."

- "Nothing I do is any good. I'll never amount to anything."

  Don't say: "What are you saying? You're a highly respected engineer! You're blowing everything out of proportion."

  Do say: "I know it's upsetting when things don't work out the way you want them to. Failure feelings are really painful. We'll get through this together."

- "How long am I going to feel this way? It feels as if I'll never get better."

  Don't say: "C'mon, nothing lasts forever. You know better than that."

  Do say: "I know it's scary to be in so much pain. Feelings come and go. We'll get through this together."[2]

9. If your friend loses interest in activities she normally enjoys, you can gently remind her of the past enjoyment that she derived from the activities and then firmly *encourage her to become involved again.* Don't ask her if she would like to, as she might not know or care to respond. Don't get angry and say, "You're going with me because I'm sick and tired of you

sitting around feeling sorry for yourself." You could say, "I know that you haven't felt well in the past, but I feel that you are entitled to some enjoyment. I think you might like this once we get started. And I would like to share this activity with you."

By getting involved, the person begins to break the destructive behavior patterns, and this helps her gain energy and motivation. One of the best things to do is to keep your friend busy. Physical activity in severe depression can be more beneficial than mental activity. The activities planned should be those that she has enjoyed in the past, with all preparations made in detail.

10. If your friend begins to let her appearance go, don't hint about the situation. Openly, clearly, and explicitly *tell her that she will enjoy fixing herself up* and perhaps will feel better for it.

11. Loss of confidence and self-esteem is common in depression. *Don't ever kid, tease, or lecture her about her lack of confidence.* And don't ignore it; it must be faced. In reactivating self-esteem, help the person see the illogic of her self-disparagement, but don't do it by berating or arguing. Look for past accomplishments in her life and get her to focus upon what she was able to accomplish prior to the onset of the depression.

Don't join in the self-pity, but respond by saying, "Perhaps you can't do some things the way you did before, but let's talk about the things you still do well. What do you think they are?" If she says, "I can't do anything," gently *name some things she can do*, or draw them out of her. Be persistent and steady in your responses.

By following these principles, it is possible for us to fulfill the biblical teaching on giving empathy and encouragement to one another. Galatians 6:1 says, "Brethren, if any person is overtaken in misconduct or sin of any sort, you who are spiritual [who are responsive to and controlled by the Spirit] should set him right and restore and reinstate him, without any sense of superiority and with all gentleness, keeping an attentive eye on yourself, lest you should be tempted also" (AMP).

There will be times when a friend is struggling with worry. In fact, it helps to ask, "Do you have a tendency to worry?" Most will say, "Oh, yes," or "It's a constant battle." (To help your friend with worry, read chapters 1–3 of my book *Winning Over Your Emotions*.)

Try the following exercise—it can be very helpful.

Read Psalm 37:1–7 aloud to your friend. You might share the following: Psalm 37:1 begins, "Do not fret." The dictionary defines "fret" as "to eat away, gnaw, gall, vex, worry, agitate, wear away."

In addition to telling us not to fret, Psalm 37 gives us positive substitutes for worry. First it says, "Trust (lean on, rely on, and be confident) in the Lord" (v. 3, AMP). Trust is a matter of not attempting to live an independent life or to cope with difficulties alone. It means going to a greater source for strength.

Verse four says, "Delight yourself also in the Lord" (AMP). To delight means to rejoice in God and what He has done for us, to let God supply the joy for our life.

Verse 5 says, "Commit your way to the Lord" (AMP). Commitment is a definite act of the will, and it involves releasing our worries and anxieties to the Lord.

And finally, we are to "rest in the Lord; wait for Him" (verse 7 AMP). This means to submit in silence to what He ordains, and to be ready and expectant for what He is going to do in our life.[3]

Ask your friend to read these verses out loud several times a day as a reminder. Also ask what would assist her in applying each principle.

The next suggestion is a bit different: Say to your friend, "Tomorrow when you begin to worry about something, instead of worrying at that moment, write down what you're worried about on an index card and keep the card in your pocket. Each time a worry pops up, write it on the card, but *don't worry about it yet*. Then about 4:00 PM, go into a room where you can be alone. Sit down, take out the card, and worry about those items as intensely as you can for thirty minutes. Start the next day with a new blank card and do the same thing."[4]

The most helpful approach I've learned over the years is the "Stop/Think" approach: Suggest to your friend that she take a blank index card and on one side write the word STOP in large, bold letters. On the other side write the complete text of Philippians 4:6–9. It's interesting to note that God says *He* will guard our hearts, but *we* are to guide our minds. Ask her to keep the card with her at all times. Whenever she is alone and begins to worry, take the card out, hold the STOP side in front of her, and say aloud "Stop!" twice with emphasis. Then suggest she turn the card over and read the Scripture passage aloud twice with emphasis.

This passage states:

> *Don't worry about anything; instead pray about everything; tell God your needs, and don't forget to thank him for his answers. If you do this, you will experience God's peace, which is far more wonderful than the human mind can understand. His peace will keep your thoughts and your hearts quiet and at rest as you trust in Christ Jesus. And now, brothers, as I close this letter, let me say this one more thing: Fix your thoughts on what is true and good and right. Think about things that are pure and lovely, and dwell on the fine, good things in others. Think about all you can praise God for and be glad about. Keep putting into practice all you learned from me and saw me doing, and the God of peace will be with you.* (TLB)

Resources

Dark Clouds, Silver Linings, Archibald Hart (Focus on the Family, 1993).
Seeing in the Dark, Gary Kinnaman and Richard Jacobs, MD (Bethany House, 2006).

When the Blues Won't Go Away: New Approaches to Dysthymic Disorder and Other Forms of Chronic Low-Grade Depression, Robert Hirschfield, MD (MacMillan, 1991).

When Feeling Bad Is Good, Ellen McGraw (Henry Holt, 1992).

Winning Over Your Emotions, H. Norman Wright (Harvest House, 1998).

Say It in Writing

CHAPTER 10

IF THERE IS ANYTHING THAT HELPS a hurting person more than spoken words it is written words. I know. Following the death of our son, we received so many written expressions of comfort. And this went on for six or seven years—that's what helped so much. But while *we* continued to receive written words of comfort, most people don't.

Most who are hurting receive an abundance of cards and notes at first, during a time when their pain is so great the words of comfort may not register as much as they would later on. Write reminders on your calendar to *send notes every three to four months for at least two years.* All it takes is one person doing this; your act of caring sends the message, "Your loss is not forgotten." And remember, losses are not confined to deaths.

Perhaps the most important part of sending a note is to put it in your own handwriting. A typed note or one purchased that you only sign doesn't convey the same message as one in your own handwriting. Many letters that you write will be kept and reread for years.

Writing letters and notes to a hurting friend is not easy. In fact, for many the most challenging letter to write is a letter of condolence. How can you craft a simple expression of words on a page that can penetrate the pain of loss and grief and bring support and care to a friend's heart and mind? We don't want to be superficial or stilted in our expression. So it's easy to postpone writing to the extent we never do it, even though we wanted to reach out in this way.

Listen to your feelings of compassion and care, then simply translate those feelings into your own words. Here are some specific suggestions that may help you.

Guidelines for Writing a Condolence Letter or Card

The following can give you some structure, but these are just suggestions. You can change any of them to make your expressions more appropriate to the loss your friend has experienced.

The first component of a letter is to *acknowledge* the loss. If someone other than your friend informed you, let him know how you learned about his loss. It's all right to express your feelings about hearing of the loss. You can say you were shocked or stunned or taken aback by the news. If the loss was a person, mention him by name. This can apply to a death, a divorce, or the breakup of a relationship.

> Dear _____,
>
> I was taken aback today when John called to tell me that your father had died. It seemed so sudden and must have been a shock to you.

Express your *concern*. Let your friend know that you care and in some way connect with his sense of loss. If you know the person who died (or left or otherwise was involved in the loss for your friend), share your sadness. And use the appropriate words. If it was a death, use the word. If it was a betrayal or a suicide, use those words.

> It's hard to find the words to convey my love and concern for you over the untimely death of your father. I wish I could help fill that empty spot you have in your life at this time. I miss him too, as well as the ongoing stories you always recount to me. Those are a loss as well.

It helps to make note of *special qualities of the person who died*. This can be done whether you knew him personally or just through the stories of your friend. In doing this, you're reminding your friend that the person he lost made a contribution and was appreciated.

> *I remember the times I spent time with you and your father. He was a gracious man and showed interest in what I was involved in. He made me feel a part of your family.*

It helps to *share a special memory* you have of the one who died. This can help your friend, since his shock and grief have short-circuited his ability to remember details. When you share your memory, tell what made it special to you. It could be serious or humorous.

> *I remember one time when you invited me to a barbecue. Remember what your dad did to those porterhouse steaks? They were turned into charcoal when he got distracted. His sense of humor and willingness to go buy some more instead of getting upset impressed me so much. He really was special.*

In addition to memories, it's helpful to *mention special qualities about your friend*. This is a time when he is so overwhelmed that he may question his own capabilities. Bring out any traits that helped him deal with past adversities. And if you can remember any words or affirmations the deceased made about your friend, he needs to hear those now.

> *This is going to be a difficult journey for you. It's not the first one you've been on. I've seen your strength and determination in adversity before. I remember your dad saying you were not only a survivor but a person who could take difficult times and use them, not only for your growth but also to bless others. In time this will occur again.*

Part of your letter will be to *offer assistance* to your friend if you're able to do so. But whatever you offer, be sure you can follow through. Don't say, "Let me know if there's anything I can do." It's hard for your friend to think, let alone ask for help. Take the lead and suggest two or three specific tasks that you could do, such as shopping, running errands, cleaning, or making phone calls.

> *I want to help you in the best way possible. I have some ideas so I'll call Saturday after you've had some time and we can talk about them at that time.*[1]

When you close your letter, do so with a thoughtful word or phrase. This is another time to *reflect your feelings*. There are many expressions to use:

> *Our love is with you always.*
> *You are in my thoughts and prayers.*
> *You know you have my deepest sympathy and my love and friendship always.*
> *My thoughts are with you now, and I send you my deepest sympathy.*
> *We all join in sending you our heartfelt love.*[2]

What about sharing your own grief experiences? This can be done if you've had a similar loss experience, but *don't compare* the two. The worst and most anger-producing phrase we can use is, "I know (understand) exactly how you feel." No you don't. None of us do, since grief and loss are so very personal. You could, however, share the depth of your pain and how you survived.

Future notes don't have to be long. They can be brief and to the point.

Hi, I was having my prayer time and your face came to mind. How are you really doing today? Hope you're eating and sleeping. I'll call about having a breakfast. Love you.

Share the Word of God

When you find yourself struggling with what to say, Scripture verses, including the following, can be helpful:

The eternal God is your Refuge, and underneath are the everlasting arms. (Deuteronomy 33:27 TLB)

When you go through deep waters and great trouble, I will be with you. When you go through rivers of difficulty, you will not drown! When you walk through the fire of oppression, you will not be burned up—the flames will not consume you. For I am the Lord your God, your Savior, the Holy One of Israel. . . . Don't be afraid, for I am with you. (Isaiah 43:2–3, 5 TLB)

For I am persuaded, that neither death, nor life, nor angels, nor principalities, nor powers, nor things present, nor things to come, nor height, nor depth, nor any other creature, shall be able to separate us from the love of God, which is in Christ Jesus our Lord. (Romans 8:38–39 KJV)

Even though I walk through the valley of the shadow of death, I will fear no evil: for thou art with me; thy rod and thy staff they comfort me. (Psalm 23:4 KJV)

He heals the brokenhearted. . . . (Psalm 147:3 NASB)

He hath said, I will never leave thee, nor forsake thee. (Hebrews 13:5 KJV)

Do not fear, for I am with you; do not be dismayed, for I am your God. I will strengthen you and help you; I will uphold you. (Isaiah 41:10)

When I pray, you answer me, and encourage me by giving

me the strength I need. (Psalm 138:3 TLB)

Be strong and courageous, do not be afraid . . . for the Lord your God is the one who goes with you. He will not fail you or forsake you. (Deuteronomy 31:6 NASB)

Quotations Can Help

Personal notes that include quotes that are selected with sensitivity for the specific person in mind take a little extra time and thought, but the healing effect they may have on a grief-stricken friend is well worth the effort. Sources for short, comforting quotes are almost limitless. One little book full of words of wisdom that will turn weakness into strength is *When Sorrow Comes,* by Robert Ozment. Here's a passage from that book that has been shared with those in despair:

> *I wish I had a magic word to wipe away your tears! I do not know any magic words, but I know a God who can heal you and I commend Him to you. Remember, the door of death is the only door that leads to the Father's house. He will be waiting there to greet and welcome His children.*[3]

Peter Marshall, the legendary Scottish chaplain of the United States Senate in the late 1940s, died at age forty-six. Uncanny as it seems, he was reported to have spoken words befitting his own eulogy: "The measure of a life, after all, is not its duration, but its donation." When the death of a younger person occurs, these words may be appropriately incorporated into a personal note.

Quotes included in notes do not have to be spoken by famous people. The main criterion is that the quote is something that *helps soothe the hurt* caused by the death of a loved one.

Helen Steiner Rice had a special gift of expressing emotions felt by grieving persons. Books of her poems are in most libraries.

There are times when you can include poems, quotes, or Scripture. At other times prayers are appropriate to use in your letters or notes. Some examples are:

> *When the joy of living is lost, O God, and life becomes a long weariness, kindle again the light that has failed, and the love that will not let me go.*[4]

> *Lord, when sometimes my life in this world seems too much to bear, help me to claim Your wonderful promise of victory over tears, death, sorrow and pain. I thank You that all things are made new through You and that I will share in Your kingdom.*[5]

> *I am empty, Father. I am bitter, even toward You. I grieve, not only for the one I have lost, but for the loving part of myself that seems to have died as well. You, Who have at other times brought the dead back to life, revive my dead ability to love, to be close, to care about this world and those I know. I believe, I insist, that You can heal this mortal wound.*[6]

Sample Letters

The following sample letters may assist you in creating your own. Letter from an adult to an adult:

Dear Wendy and Spencer,

The news of your mother's death, while not unexpected, was nevertheless a blow. The final word is so definite always. I want to express my deep sympathy, but also, I feel a quiet understanding that your beloved mother—who suffered long—has finally found release. I can only imagine what the loss means to you and the rest of the family. You can all take great comfort from the fact that each and every one of you did everything possible—far beyond the call of duty—to make your mother's last troublesome days as easy for her as possible. She loved her family and knew that they loved her.

Dorothy's friends know how extraordinary a woman she was, as a wife, as a mother, as a friend, and as a co-worker. She has left her mark on us and we know that we have lost a great friend whose life was a pattern to guide us and an inspiration to live by. May God comfort you and ease your pain.[7]

Letter from an adult to a child:

Dear Jimmy,

Today I heard that your dad died just a few hours after the terrible accident. You feel awful and like your world is turned upside down. All of us feel sad because your dad was such a neat man. He meant so much to us too.

Your life will be different in the next few weeks and months. Sometimes sadness makes us feel angry and confused. All of you in your family really need one another's love. It may be hard, but it helps to talk about your sadness. It may help to draw or write about your feelings.

We all love you very much. I will call you real soon.

Letter upon the death of a spouse:

Dear Kim,

For the past day, my thoughts have been of nothing but you and the beautiful Julia. I don't know if there's anything that can be said to soften the pain of your grief just now, but my love, my unqualified friendship, and my prayers are with you.

Julia was such a vibrant spirit. Her exuberance made life

around her a constant adventure. You joined her on that adventure with all your heart, whether sailing through the islands or sitting silently by a mountain stream. There was a sense among many who knew you that you each embraced fully the unknowable mystery that is life. I guess the mystery just gets deeper.

I'm reminded of a short piece by Henry Van Dyke. It's called "A Parable of Immortality":

"I am standing upon the seashore. A ship at my side spreads her white sails to the morning breeze and starts for the blue ocean. She is an object of beauty and strength, and I stand and watch until at last she hangs like a speck of white cloud just where the sea and sky come down to mingle with each other. Then someone at my side says, 'There she goes!'

"Gone where? Gone from my sight . . . that is all. She is just as large in mast and hull and spar as she was when she left my side and just as able to bear her load of living freight to the place of destination. Her diminished size is in me, not in her. And just at the moment when someone at my side says, 'There she goes!' there are other eyes watching her coming and other voices ready to take up the glad shout, 'Here she comes!'"

So, Alex, may the winds of life blow gently around you at this difficult time. I want to help in any way I'm able. I'll call Thursday.

In trust and friendship.[8]

If the loss was traumatic in some way, you may struggle with what to say. Grief is intensified if there was no opportunity to say good-bye, like in the case of accidents, fatal heart attacks, homicide, suicide, etc. Often when a death occurs in this way there is an intensity of feelings that can include regrets, guilt, shame, anger, or rejection. There is the reaction of shock as well as the feeling of senselessness.

The following is a letter to the parents of a young woman who was murdered:

> *Dear Dr. and Mrs. Rodriguez,*
>
> *It is with feelings of profound distress that we heard the very sad news of your daughter's death under such tragic circumstances. Her untimely passing is a most severe and grievous loss. There is no sense to it on Earth; we can only look to Jesus, Our Lord.*
>
> *"Cast your cares on the Lord and he will sustain you"* (Psalm 55:22).
>
> *We want to express our own deep sadness. Perhaps no words that we say will ease the pain, anguish, or emptiness that you feel in your hearts, but we want you to know that we will remember your daughter as a graceful, loving and open-hearted girl who brightened the neighborhood with her smile.*
>
> *It may seem impossible now, but while nothing will ever bring Eileen back, we hope that one day you will find a source of comfort in beautiful memories of the years of joy God gave you together.*
>
> *May God bless you and keep you.*[9]

When our retarded son, Matthew, died in 1990 at the age of twenty-two (mentally he was about eighteen months old), we received an outpouring of cards and letters from scores of people. We kept them, as they contain so many significant memories. Since Matt lived at a special facility for the disabled the last eleven years of his life, some of the letters came from those who cared for him. Many contained a special experience they had with Matthew that we didn't know about. These experiences gave us new insights as well as memories about him, which have become very important. Even though you may think some experience might be trivial, to a bereaved parent it becomes special. I was comforted and felt loved by those who wrote.

Let me close this chapter with portions of several letters we received:

Dear Norm,

I just heard this morning of the death of your son, Matthew. I want you to know of our personal grieving for you and our prayers for you and your family during this time. My wife and I had a son who drowned almost eight years ago and so I can somewhat identify with the sense of loss that you are feeling. Please rest assured of our continued support and love for you as a Christian brother.

Dear Norm and Joyce,

Thank you for letting us know that Matthew has gone home to be with the Lord.

Our hearts are saddened for you as we know a little piece of your heart seems to be missing with Matthew's death—but we send our sympathy and love, hoping to help fill that hole a little bit.

Dr. and Mrs. Wright,

I am so sorry to hear of the death of your son, Matthew. My wife and I lost a daughter about two years ago. And, my wife has a brother with Down's syndrome who's thirty-seven. So in a couple of respects I can identify to some degree with your grief.

Unfortunately, too many in the world don't understand the joy a mentally handicapped child can bring, even when the child has grown into adulthood. And so, I would imagine not everyone really knows how much you must be missing Matthew.

Pray for Your Friend

CHAPTER 11

WITH THE RING OF THE PHONE one morning I found myself speaking to a thirty-two-year-old man who was concerned about his forthcoming marriage. As we talked he told me he wanted to marry this woman he had been going with for over a year. He had made a commitment and given her the ring; now fears stemming from his childhood had begun to emerge. (This is not an uncommon situation.)

We continued to talk about the marriage and the normal concerns that most individuals have concerning this major life step. "I feel I need prayer at this time," he concluded. "Would you seal our conversation with prayer?" And at that moment, distanced by many miles, yet very close because of the phone connection and our common relationship with Jesus Christ, I prayed for him. I asked for God's insight, direction, clarity of thought, leading, and peace to invade this brother's life.

We don't have to be face-to-face to minister to a friend in prayer. As we minister over the telephone to those who are close to us, our prayer draws them closer to relying upon the Lord, instead of relying upon themselves or us.

As I get to know counselees in my office, I share with them during the first or second session that, as part of my counseling ministry, I will pray for them each day. And I tell them I would appreciate their letting me know from time to time what they would like me to pray about in their lives. Many of them are taken aback that someone would do this, but over the years many have said that *knowing one person was praying for them kept them going*.

Praying accomplishes several things. It releases our friend to God and reminds us that we are not the ones who are the final resource for him. We need the direct intervention of God to make a difference in that life! By keeping a list and praying for my counselees' specific needs, when they walk into my office I already know what their concerns have been the week before.

Sometimes the counselee asks, "How did you remember what we discussed? I don't ever see you taking many notes." My answer is that prayer is a reminder.

There will be times when you are stumped, as I have been, and you won't know how to proceed or what to say. It is perfectly all right to admit that: "I'm not sure where to go next or what is more pressing. Let's just stop; I would like to ask God to show me which direction to go at this time."

The core of helping others is prayer. But too little is said about prayer in counseling and too little is written about its use during the session and between sessions. This is not a chapter on what prayer is or how to pray according to this pattern or that pattern. Numerous books have been written on those topics. What I want to address is the *use of prayer as a means of healing* in the process of counseling.

Scripture and Prayer

Scripture teaches that, as we pray, we are assured of being welcomed into God's presence.

> *Therefore let us draw near with confidence to the throne of grace, so that we may receive mercy and find grace to help in time of need.* (Hebrews 4:16 NASB)

When we pray, we can call upon the Holy Spirit to guide our prayers.

In the same way the Spirit also helps our weakness; for we do not know how to pray as we should, but the Spirit Himself intercedes for us with groanings too deep for words; and He who searches the hearts knows what the mind of the Spirit is, because He intercedes for the saints according to the will of God. (Romans 8:26–27 NASB)

When we pray, we do so with confession, praise, and thanksgiving.

If we confess our sins, he is faithful and just and will forgive us our sins and purify us from all unrighteousness. (1 John 1:9)

Blessed be the God and Father of our Lord Jesus Christ, who has blessed us with every spiritual blessing in the heavenly places in Christ. (Ephesians 1:3 NASB)

Always giving thanks to God the Father for everything. (Ephesians 5:20)

One of the important principles of prayer is to rely upon the promises of God.

Ask and it will be given to you; seek and you will find; knock and the door will be opened to you. (Matthew 7:7)

For the eyes of the Lord are toward the righteous, and his ears attend to their prayer. (1 Peter 3:12 NASB)

If we ask anything according to his will, he hears us. And if we know that he hears us—whatever we ask—we know that we have what we asked of him. (1 John 5:14–15)

At times, you may discover a Bible passage that is perfect to use as a model for prayer with your friend. Here are some examples.

For those who are suffering:

Blessed be the God and Father of our Lord Jesus Christ, who according to His great mercy has caused us to be born again to a living hope.... In this you greatly rejoice, even though now for a little while, if necessary, you have been distressed by various trials, so that the proof of your faith, being more precious than gold which is perishable, even though tested by fire, may be found to result in praise and glory and honor at the revelation of Jesus Christ. (1 Peter 1:3, 6–7 NASB)

Do not be surprised at the fiery ordeal among you, which comes upon you for your testing ... but to the degree that you share the sufferings of Christ, keep on rejoicing; so that also at the revelation of His glory, you may rejoice with exultation. (1 Peter 4:12–13 NASB)

Consider it all joy, my brethren, when you encounter various trials, knowing that the testing of your faith produces endurance. (James 1:2–3 NASB)

For those who are worried:

Be anxious for nothing, but in everything by prayer and supplication with thanksgiving let your requests be made known to God. And the peace of God, which surpasses all comprehension, shall guard your hearts and your minds in Christ Jesus. Finally, brethren, whatever is true, whatever is honorable, whatever is right, whatever is pure, whatever is lovely, whatever is of good repute, if there is any excellence and if anything worthy of praise, let your mind dwell on these things. The things you have learned and received and heard and seen in me, practice these things; and the God of peace shall be with you. (Philippians 4:6–9 NASB)

For those who feel oppressed and in distress:

Answer me when I call, O God of my righteousness!
Thou hast relieved me in my distress;
Be gracious to me and hear my prayer. (Psalm 4:1 NASB)

My heart is in anguish within me,
And the terrors of death have fallen upon me.
Fear and trembling come upon me;
And horror has overwhelmed me.
I said, "Oh that I had wings like a dove!
I would fly away and be at rest.
Behold, I would wander far away,
I would lodge in the wilderness.
I would hasten to my place of refuge
From the stormy wind and tempest." . . .
I shall call upon God,
And the Lord will save me.
Evening and morning and at noon, I will complain and murmur,
And He will hear my voice.
He will redeem my soul in peace from the battle
which is against me,
For they are many who strive with me. (Psalm 55:4–8, 16–18
NASB)

Do not fear, for I have redeemed you;
I have called you by name; you are Mine!
When you pass through the waters, I will be with you;
And through the rivers, they will not overflow you.
When you walk through fire, you will not be scorched,
Nor will the flame burn you.

For I am the Lord your God, the Holy One of Israel, your Savior.
(Isaiah 43:1–3 NASB)

For those who need God's forgiveness:

Who is a God like you, who pardons sin and forgives the transgression of the remnant of his inheritance? You do not stay angry forever but delight to show mercy. You will again have compassion on us; you will tread our sins underfoot and hurl all our iniquities into the depths of the sea. (Micah 7:18–19)

Then I acknowledged my sin to you and did not cover up my iniquity. I said, "I will confess my transgressions to the Lord"— and you forgave the guilt of my sin. (Psalm 32:5)

How to Pray With Hurting People

Sometimes I ask people exactly what they would like me to pray about and allow them to direct me. On other occasions I say, "This is how I'm going to pray for you this week." There will be times when this is what keeps your friend going. And before you give this request to others or put it on a prayer chain, find out if this is all right with him. It's a way of asking, "Who do you want to know about this?"

As you pray, be sure to rely upon the Holy Spirit for instruction in how to pray. Allow Him to bring to mind through your imagination the direction needed in prayer. Too often we quickly pray with our own words, which come from our intellect. Our prayer lacks freshness because it reflects our own direction and not that of the Holy Spirit.

Be careful about asking your friend to pray. He may be angry at God or just doesn't have the words at this time. "Grief has a way of plundering our prayer life, leaving us feeling immobile and empty."[1]

Ask your friend if he would like you to pray with him or for him. Don't be intrusive and don't pray long! Keep it brief but sensitive. If you have the opportunity to pray for someone in the midst of deep difficulty, see it as a privilege. I have seen some who pray because they either don't know what to say or they're uncomfortable with silence. And some pray trying to fix or convict their friend. But your motivation should be to *bring your friend to God and His resources.*

What's the best way to pray with your friends? Let me share what Dr. Gordon MacDonald suggested at a trauma conference in New York on how to pray for those in difficulty.

There are five kinds of prayers that your friends need as an intervention during their time of difficulty.

1. Give a *prayer of encouragement.*

Encourage means to press courage into someone. *Discourage* means to suck courage out of him. Your hope, your courage, your belief in him and the future can be transferred to your friend. Ask for God to encourage your friend, to give him strength and courage. You might share with him how precious he is in God's sight. Read a Scripture such as Ephesians 1:4–6 to him:

> *Long ago, even before he made the world, God loved us and chose us in Christ to be holy and without fault in his eyes. His unchanging plan has always been to adopt us into his own family by bringing us to himself through Jesus Christ. And this gave him great pleasure. So we praise God for the wonderful kindness he has poured out on us because we belong to his dearly loved Son.* (NLT)

A prayer might be, "Oh God, my friend means so much to me and to you. I believe as you do that he has the ability and the strength to carry on in the midst of this difficulty. Give him a clear mind, a peaceful mind, and your guidance."

When a person questions whether or not God cares for him, I have shared portions of this song, an adaptation of Zephaniah 3:14, 17 and Psalm 54:2, 4:

> *And the Father will dance over you in joy!*
> *He will take delight in whom He loves.*
> *Is that a choir I hear singing the praises of God?*
> *No, the Lord God Himself is exulting over you in song!*
> *And He will joy over you in song!*
> *My soul will make its boast in God,*
> *For He has answered all my cries.*
> *His faithfulness to me is as sure as the dawn of a new day.*
> *Awake my soul, and sing!*
> *Let my spirit rejoice in God!*
> *Sing, O daughter of Zion, with all of your heart!*
> *Cast away fear for you have been restored!*
> *Put on the garment of praise as on a festival day.*
> *Join with the Father in glorious, jubilant song.*
> *God rejoices over you in song!*[2]

2. Another prayer is the *prayer of restoration*. This is for the person who has failed or thinks he has failed. He has nothing left and is exhausted. Grief has overwhelmed him. He needs someone to pray and restore a sense of grace in his life. Perhaps it's as simple as "Lord, just fill my friend with hope for today and tomorrow. May he be secure in your arms," or "Lord, help my friend to know he is loved."

Gordon MacDonald prayed for a friend in this way:

> *O Lord God, here's my friend whom I've come to love. You know how much he's hurting today, Lord. I know that he's fearful. I know that he's in physical pain. Lord, he needs something from you that no human being can give him. He needs new*

power in his life. He needs new courage in his life. He needs to know that tomorrow can be brighter than anything that's been in the past. Lord, he needs the kind of strength that only heaven can give. So, Lord, would you take my friend today? I put my hands on him so you know who he is. Would you take my friend today and bring healing to his broken life?[3]

3. A third kind of prayer is the *prayer of affirmation.* That's the prayer in which you recognize something in your friend that he cannot see in himself.

Lord, I thank you for the way my friend is making such good decisions this past week and the way he continues to _____. We see what you are doing in his life.

When you pray a prayer of affirmation for your friend, you are building value and confidence that God wants him to have. In doing this you're a "balcony person." You're leaning out of the balcony and saying, "Yes, you can do it. You're capable. See what you've already done. Wow!"

Be affirming in both your prayers and your comments.

4. There is also a *prayer of blessing,* in which you pronounce upon another person what you know is God's purpose and will for him. You find this within the Scriptures again and again.

The Lord bless you and keep you; the Lord make his face shine upon you and be gracious to you; the Lord turn his face toward you and give you peace. (Numbers 6:24–26)

What could you say?

Blessed be the God and Father of our Lord Jesus Christ. May He bless you with _____.

May the Lord bless you and keep you strong....

May the Lord give you hope that will neither despair nor disappoint....

5. Last is the *prayer of intercession.* This is called for when your friend is so weak and needy that you need to stand between him and God, praying on his behalf. In John 17 Jesus intercedes for His disciples. At times we are called to pray for others too. You will know what is needed as you listen to what your friend says to you.

You could pray the following:

Father, sometimes events intrude into our lives that bring distress and discouragement. Use your Word and the work of your Holy Spirit to lift this from my friend and bring comfort. I thank you in advance for doing this. In Jesus' name I pray.

Dear God, my friend needs the Holy Spirit as the Great Comforter at this moment to overcome the pain and distress.

Be simple in your prayers. Be short. Be sincere. And if you promise to pray, write yourself a reminder so you are faithful. Let your friend know that you've been praying.

You can never fully understand the power of prayer in your hurting friend's life.

What to Do—What Not to Do

CHAPTER 12

ONE OF YOUR FRIENDS might come to you with a problem you've never encountered before. And you will wonder, *What should I say? How should I respond?*

As Christians, we have an opportunity to share Christ's love by the way we reach out to comfort and support others when they have endured a loss. But there are guidelines for us to follow in reacting to the grief of a friend or relative. A number of suggestions have already been given throughout this book. Some will be reiterated here because they are so important, and some new guidelines will be discussed as well.

Helping the Terminally Ill

Most people find it hard to know what to say to a person who's been diagnosed as having a terminal illness. Often they say nothing, which makes them appear uncaring. If you have heard that your friend has a terminal illness, open your conversation by saying, "I understand you've been ill lately." *Then take your cues from the person.* If she wants to talk about it, she will. Tune in to her feelings and respond not just to what is said but to her nonverbal communication as well. If she chooses not to discuss her illness, then it's her choice. At least you've acknowledged her illness and let her know you care about her.

"The ill person often thinks that friends are going to think less of them because they're ill. The patient thinks, 'They're going to see me undesirable as a friend.' People don't want to deal with it because they have to think about the possibility of their own death. They don't know what to say, so they avoid [saying anything]."[1]

Not knowing what to say is probably the most common and frustrating feeling we experience when a friend or loved one is going through a loss experience. We all struggle with what to say, how to say it, and when to respond. But it is possible to learn how to minister to others in a way that is supportive and caring.

The "Do Nots"

Here are four major "do nots" you need to know. (1) Do not withdraw from the relative or friend. (2) Do not compare, evaluate, or judge the person or her responses. (3) Do not look for sympathy for yourself. (4) Do not patronize or pity the person.

In any loss, a person needs continuing, ongoing support from a number of people. As mentioned before, our support is often given disproportionately—lots at first and very little later on. One woman remarked, "Few people call now. I'm very lonely. No one worries about my meals or how I am managing my time. People suddenly disappeared, assuming I'm fully recovered from my loss. I'm not recovered. My loneliness now seems even worse. I'm embarrassed that I miss feeling *special*."[2]

The bereaved individual needs comfort on a consistent basis. She needs to be able to talk about what has occurred and reminisce. In both death and divorce there are major decisions that need to be made. In all types of loss a support group may be needed immediately. (See the recommendations at the end of the book.)

When you see your friend or relative, the most basic response is to ask how the person is doing and feeling. A simple, "How are you doing? It's been ten days since you lost _____. How are you feeling?" will open the door. The important thing then is to let the person talk without feeling that you're comparing, evaluating, or judging.

The third "do not" involves eliciting sympathy for yourself. It sounds strange, but it does happen. Some people talk more about their own sense of loss and grief in an effort to express their sorrow and empathy. But you cannot expect the other person to help you at this time. This is a time for you to give, not receive. If you need assistance, get it from somebody else.

Have you ever felt patronized by another person? Then you know it leaves you feeling dependent and childlike. You begin to wallow in self-pity and feel worse than before you interacted with the "helpful" person.

The "Do's"

There are several positive guidelines—or "do's"—to follow in ministering to a friend, relative, or neighbor. The first step is simply *accepting what has happened and how she is responding*. You may have your own perspective as to what your friend should be doing or how she should be responding, but you are not an authority on that individual's responses, so you will need to revise your expectations.

Accept her and let her know her feelings are normal. Some are going to apologize to you for their tears, depression, or anger. You will hear comments like, "I can't believe I'm still crying like this. I'm so sorry." "I don't know why I'm so upset." "I know I shouldn't be angry, but I guess I really am."

You can be an encourager by accepting her feelings. Give her the gift of facing her feelings and expressing them. Here are some statements that you can make to your friend who is sad:

"I don't want you to worry about crying in front of me. It's hard to feel this sad and not express it in tears. You may find me crying with you at times."

"I hope you feel the freedom to express your sorrow in tears in front of me. I won't be embarrassed or upset. I just want to be here with you."

"If I had experienced what you have been through, I would feel like opening my eyes and letting the flood of tears come pouring out. Do you ever feel like that?"

Anger is another feeling that is difficult for many people to express. Use comments like:

"It is natural to feel anger and hostility toward everyone and everything that had to do with your husband's death. I feel angry too."

"You must be very angry that your baby has suffered and you can do nothing about it."

"It is normal and reasonable to be angry and resentful when you have lost your baby while others have healthy babies."

"It must be hard to find the words to express your anger, helplessness, and frustration."

"It is important that you allow yourself to express your anger and rage no matter how much others try to discourage you."[3]

Your encouragement to express feelings will help the grieving person understand that her expression will not cause you to withdraw from her. Reassure her that you are not going to leave because of her feelings or try to talk her out of feeling the way she does.

Another positive way of responding is with *touch*. But be sensitive to the person you're ministering to—she may not be as comfortable with touch as you are. If she seems to reject your physical gestures like hugs or a hand on the shoulder, be sure to respect her. If you extend a hand and she stiffens up, it's a good indication that your brief words and physical presence will help more than touch. In time she may come to you and say, "I need a hug."

Many people you minister to *will* need touch, since for many people, touching eases the emptiness of the inner pain. A widow expresses her feelings in this way:

> *Your mind is still on crutches.... There is something awe-inspiring, silencing, and shattering about emotional pain that*

does leave one at a loss for words. Perhaps gestures are better. I've mentioned before my need for hugs. I'm sure other people feel the same way. Human physical comfort, no strings. I saw a cartoon once, no caption. . . . It was [on a] vending machine; the sign on it read: "Hugs 25 cents." I wish I could have one installed.[4]

In his delightful book *Just a Touch of Nearness,* Fred Bauer tells this story:

I once heard about the tragic traffic death of a young child. Nancy, just six years old, had been struck by a speeding car. Her parents were devastated. So were her schoolmates, especially Joyce, Nancy's closest friend. As soon as Joyce heard the news about Nancy, she wanted to run to her friend's house. But Joyce's mother thought it would be too upsetting for their daughter and for Nancy's parents. "Daddy and you and I will go to the funeral," she consoled. "You can see Nancy's parents there." But a tearful Joyce insisted that she must see them immediately.

What worried Joyce's mother was what she herself might say to the grieving parents. But finally, reluctantly, she agreed to take her daughter to Nancy's house. And when they arrived, Joyce ran to her lost friend's mother, climbed up on her lap, and threw her arms around her. Wordlessly, the two of them cried out their mutual hurt.

No one who came to say, "I'm sorry," said it better than Joyce.[5]

The Gift of Listening

One of the greatest gifts that you can give to a hurting, grieving person is the gift of listening, which I've already talked about. When people know you hear them, they will trust you and feel safe with you. If you are a good listener, others will be more apt to invite you into their lives. Those you listen to will also learn through your example to respond openly and lovingly to what others share with them.

Nurturing listening is very important in helping your friend. In this type of listening, you listen for the emotional content behind the message being shared and empathetically reflect it to the speaker in your own words. Nurturing listening conveys support, caring, and acceptance for the person and his or her point of view. It extends a warm invitation to the griever to share his deepest joys, concerns, or hurts with you.

As you listen you are going to hear the same thoughts expressed again and again. Grieving people, whether it be the loss of a pet, a job, a home, a pregnancy, or a person, have a compelling need to retell the details of their loss. They want to talk about the who, what, when, and how. The details vary depending on the nature of the loss. Do you remember why a person tends to focus so much on the details, and in some cases, final conversations with someone they lost? It gives her an opportunity to hold on to whatever she lost. Don't be put off by the details of the story even though you may know them by heart. This telling of details goes on until she is assured that she will not lose the memory of the person she lost. When she reaches that point, the clinging to exacting details will lessen.

When grieving people give the details, encourage them to express the accompanying feelings as well. Their feelings will be relieved as you listen without shock, embarrassment, or judgment.

Often in the case of an accident, loss of an important position, or death you will hear the person *taking responsibility* for what occurred, even when she had no responsibility or could not have done anything about what happened. This is an opportunity for you to say something like: "What could you have done to prevent that from happening? Would that really have been possible? Is there anyone else who could have done anything? If so, why didn't they? I can see how you might feel that way, but there really was nothing that any of us could have done." Before you make statements such as these, help them identify all of the "if only" and "regret" statements they may have.

Above all, don't say too much to the hurting person. Your presence speaks volumes. Joseph Bayly wrote a book many years ago called *The Last Thing We Talk About*. It is the story of how he and his wife coped with the deaths of three of their sons. He gave this advice:

> *Sensitivity in the presence of grief should usually make us more silent, more listening. "I'm sorry" is honest; "I know how you feel" is usually not—even though you may have experienced the death of a person who had the same familial relationship to you as the deceased person had to the grieving one. If the person feels that you can understand, he'll tell you. Then you may want to share your own honest, not prettied-up feelings in your personal aftermath with death. Don't try to "prove" anything to a survivor. An arm around the shoulder, a firm grip of the hand, a kiss: these are the proofs grief needs, not logical reasoning. I was sitting, torn by grief. Someone came and talked to me of God's dealings, of why it happened, of hope beyond the grave. He talked constantly, he said things I knew were true. I was unmoved, except to wish he would go away. He finally did. Another came and sat beside me. He didn't ask leading questions. He just sat beside me for an hour and more, listened when I said something, answered briefly, prayed simply, left, I was moved. I was comforted. I hated to see him go.[6]*

Patience: A Necessary Character Quality

If there is one character quality that is necessary in ministering to a grieving person, it is patience. You will hear the same story with the same details and see the same tears again and again. This is both normal and necessary. What may be quite uncomfortable for you is to see anger expressed. It may make you want to say, "Enough!" But remind yourself that it's a natural and healthy response if it is within reasonable bounds.

You may even become the *target* for your friend's anger. If she withdraws from you, don't push her. This is part of grief. It's as though she moves in and out of the real world. She will progress at her pace, not yours. The author of *Beyond Grief* describes the process so well:

> No schedule exists for healing. A survivor is raw with grief and must endure much pain before healing takes place. The only course you can take is to avoid appearing restless or annoyed with the survivor.
>
> It may be difficult for you to achieve a balance between acknowledging the loss *that caused the survivor pain, and* maintaining proper perspective *in the face of that loss. You cannot help the survivor by blocking reality or steering a survivor away from painful reminders of the loss, but at the same time, you need to maintain a positive perspective while facilitating grief.*
>
> You can do this by validating the person who died, talking about how the person touched or enriched the lives of other people. When the opportunity arises, mention facets of life in which the survivor has formerly shown interest. Make a mental list of those activities or people who gave the survivor enjoyment. By doing this you are indicating to the survivor that there has been a past *and* there will be a future *with these same things, people and places in it.*[7]

Practical Help

There are many practical things you can do to help in any type of loss. I hope you will begin to respond to all of the losses people experience, some of which don't have much social recognition or support. Any major loss cuts deeply, whether it is divorce, personal rejection, job loss, or death.

With each loss you will need to (1) discover your friend's personal situation and needs; (2) decide what you are willing and able to do for her; and (3) contact her and offer to do the most difficult of the jobs you've chosen. If your friend rejects your offer, suggest another. Specific tasks could include feeding pets, making and delivering meals, doing yard work, making difficult phone calls, obtaining needed information regarding support groups or new employment, providing transportation, being available to run errands, and so forth. At some point in time, giving her a sensitive, supportive book on loss and grief could be helpful.[8]

If the loss affected one person, minister to that person. But if it affected the family unit, there needs to be ministry to each family member, both adults and children. I've heard many husbands say, "I'm so tired of people asking how my wife is doing. For once I wish they'd ask how I'm doing."

In deciding how you can minister to others, you'll find the following guidelines helpful. They are taken from the book *What to Say When You Don't Know What to Say* by Lauren Briggs.

What Not to Do

Don't try to minimize your friend's pain with comments like, "It's probably for the best." "Things could be worse." "You'll remarry." "You're young, you can always have another one." "You're strong, you'll get over it soon." "You know God is in control." Comments like these might be an attempt to offer hope, but to a hurting person, they sound as though you don't comprehend the enormity of what's happened. They don't acknowledge their pain and loss.

What It's Best to Do

You can offer simple, understanding statements such as: "This must be very hard for you." "I share your feelings of loss." "I wish I could take the hurt away." Comments like these let the person know you acknowledge their pain and that it's okay for them to feel that way.

What Not to Do

Don't say, "I'm so sorry," and end the sentence. Your hurting friend is probably sorry too, but he can't respond to that kind of comment.

What It's Best to Do

Say, "I'm so sorry." Then add, "I know how special he was to you." "I'll miss her also." "I want to help you; I'm available any time you need me." "I've been praying for you. Is there something specific I should be praying for?"

What Not to Do

Don't just say, "Is there anything I can do to help?"

What It's Best to Do

Be aggressive with your willingness to help. Ask yourself, *What would I need if I were in a similar situation?* Offer specific things you can do for her, like, "I'm on my way to the store. What can I pick up for you?" "Would your children like to come over and play this afternoon?" Most of the time, a person in a crisis can't decide what she does need. Besides, she probably doesn't want to impose.

What Not to Do

Don't say, "You shouldn't feel that way."

What It's Best to Do

Encourage her to write down her thoughts and feelings. Often, just seeing her thoughts on paper helps her deal with what she is facing.

What Not to Do

Do not try to answer her questions of "Why?" You don't have any answers and at this time even the true answer may not be apparent to her.

Job's friends didn't help with their responses, and Job said, "Miserable comforters are you all!" (Job 16:2).

What It's Best to Do

Simply answer, "I don't know why. I guess both of us would like to have some answers at this time. You would especially. I wish I had an answer to give you."

What Not to Do

Don't offer spiritual answers as to why she's facing this problem or tell her that she'll be a stronger person afterward. We don't know why tragedies happen—why certain people have to go through such trauma.

What It's Best to Do

Agree when she expresses her feelings. Say, "Yes, what happened to you isn't fair and doesn't make any sense," whether or not you share the same perspective.

What Not to Do

Don't put timetables on your hurting friend's recovery. Your inference that she's not coping well or should be her old self by now only hinders her progress. Everyone is different and recovery varies.

What It's Best to Do

Allow her all the time she needs to deal effectively with all the phases of her grief.

What Not to Do

Don't quote Bible verses as a way to correct or minimize someone's feelings. Think very carefully, asking yourself if a passage will communicate comfort or condemnation. Never offer spiritual suggestions from a position of superiority or self-righteousness.

Helping Those Who Hurt

What It's Best to Do

Give spiritual encouragement from your heart, and include Bible verses that have comforted you at a difficult time. Let her know you will pray for her daily. If you pray with her, keep it brief, reflecting her feelings in the prayer and focusing upon God's understanding of her pain and the fact that He will be her source of comfort.

What Not to Do

Don't say "I understand" when you haven't faced the same situation. Telling someone that everything will be all right when you have never known the depth of her hardship is an empty statement. And she doesn't need to hear horror stories of people you know who have been through something similar.

What It's Best to Do

Be honest about your experiences. If you haven't endured her particular kind of tragedy, say, "I haven't been through what you're facing, but I want you to know I care about you and will support you through the difficult time ahead." If you've had a similar crisis, tell her about it briefly, adding that you can empathize with her feelings.

What Not to Do

Don't expect unrealistic optimism or levity from your hurting friend.

What It's Best to Do

Realize that her heart is full of pain and turmoil. Let her know that you will listen to her feelings and you want to help her through that pain.

What Not to Do

Don't offer clichés or be unrealistically optimistic to cover up your insecurities.

What It's Best to Do

Indicate your love by saying, "I really feel awkward because I'm not sure what to say, what you need, or how to help you, but I want you to know that I love you. I'm praying for you and I'm available."

What Not to Do

Don't use "shoulds" or "if onlys" such as: "You should give the clothes away." "You should go back to work and get over this." "You should have more faith." "If only you had watched him more carefully." "If only you hadn't been so strict."

What It's Best to Do

Allow hurting people to make the decisions and take the necessary steps to deal with the trauma. No one can tell another how they should feel.

What Not to Do

Don't offer unasked-for advice. If your suggestions weren't solicited they may not be appreciated.

What It's Best to Do

Respond cautiously and prayerfully with uplifting and edifying ideas when your friend asks for your help. Let her know that you pray for her daily. On occasion, ask how she would like you to be praying for her.[9]

Be careful about saying, "This must be God's will." Rather, let your friend know that God is present with her in this suffering even if she doesn't sense Him, and He is the Comforter and Protector in the midst of pain and tragedy.

As you have walked through your own losses, you will be better able to help others walk through their valleys of loss. The walk can be so lonely when it is undertaken alone. But when others come along to just be there, listen, weep, and comfort through their presence, grievers are sustained.

None of us walks alone. Jesus Christ has been there and He is with us all of the time to sustain, encourage, and support us. Yes, life is full of losses, but Jesus Christ makes it possible to conquer them.

Grief Support Groups

IDEALLY YOUR CHURCH will have an ongoing grief recovery group. Even very small churches have found it possible to develop this type of ministry for their congregations as well as the needs of the community.

GriefShare is a program established in churches across the United States. This material provides resources for a thirteen-week grief recovery seminar/support group. A church is equipped with a video session for each meeting, a leader's guide, a leader-equipping video, and workbooks for group participants. Qualified lay people can lead this program. All the content needed is within the material. GriefShare videos feature interviews with thirty leading authors, speakers, counselors, and pastors with broad expertise in grief recovery from a biblical, Christ-centered perspective. For information on establishing a support group in your church or finding an existing one, call 1-800-875-7560, or go to *www.hnormanwright.com*.

DivorceCare is a similar type of program with videos and workbooks. Call 1-800-875-7560.

Additional Support Group Organizations:

The Compassionate Friends
(For parents who have lost children)
www.compassionatefriends.org
P.O. Box 3696
Oak Brook, IL 60522-3696
877-969-0010

Parents of Murdered Children

www.pomc.com
100 E. 8th St., Suite B-41
Cincinnati, OH 45202
888-818-POMC
513-345-4489 (fax)

Tragedy Assistance Program for Survivors (TAPS)

(Provides help for those who lose family members to military deaths)

www.taps.org
1621 Connecticut Avenue, NW, #300
Washington, DC 20009
800-959-TAPS

National Hospice and Palliative Care Organization

(For information on locating hospice services in your area, click on Find a Provider)

www.nhpco.org
1700 Diagonal Road, Suite 625
Arlington, VA 22314
800-658-8898 (help line)

Endnotes

CHAPTER 1

1. Harold Ivan Smith, *When You Don't Know What to Say* (Kansas City, MO: Beacon Hill Press, 2002), 15.
2. Nina Herrmann Donnelley, *I Never Know What to Say* (New York: Ballantine Books, 1987), 21–22.
3. Ibid., 17–24.
4. Smith, *When You Don't Know What to Say*, 7.

CHAPTER 2

1. Frederick Buechner, *Peculiar Treasures: A Biblical Who's Who* (New York: Harper & Row, 1979), 65.
2. Charlotte E. Thompson, *Raising a Handicapped Child* (New York: Morrow, 1986), 38–41.
3. Mary Ann Froehlich and PeggySue Wells, *What to Do When You Don't Know What to Say* (Minneapolis, MN: Bethany House, 2000), 98–99.
4. Ibid., 97–98.
5. Ibid., 96–97.
6. Ibid., 95.
7. Betty Jane Wylie, *The Survival Guide for Widows* (New York: Ballantine Books, 1982), 115.
8. Erin Linn, *I Know Just How You Feel: Avoiding the Clichés of Grief* (Cary, IL: Publishers Mark, 1986), xii-xiii.
9. Written by Rita Moran, *Compassionate Friends* newsletter.

CHAPTER 3

1. Harold Kushner, *Living a Life That Matters,* 123–124. Quoted in Harold Ivan Smith, *When You Don't Know What to Say* (Kansas City, MO: Beacon Hill Press, 2002), 11.

CHAPTER 4

1. Therese A. Rando, *Grieving: How to Go on Living When Someone You Love Dies* (Lexington, MA: Lexington Books, 1988), 556–557.
2. Ibid., 44.
3. Therese A. Rando, *Treatment of Complicated Mourning* (Champaign, IL: Research Press, 1983), 512.
4. Glen W. Davidson, *Understanding Mourning* (Minneapolis: Augsburg Publishing House, 1984), 59.

CHAPTER 5

1. Charles Swindoll, *Growing Strong in the Seasons of Life* (Portland, OR: Multnomah, 1983), 274–275.
2. H. Norman Wright, *Crisis Counseling* (Ventura, CA: Regal Books, 1993), chapter 1.

CHAPTER 6

1. Donald Meichenbaum, *A Clinical Handbook/Practical Therapist Manual for Assessing and Treating Adults With Post-Traumatic Stress Disorder (PTSD)* (Waterloo, Ont.: Institute Press, 1994), adapted, 23.
2. Sandra L. Brown, *Counseling Victims of Violence* (Alexandria, VA: American Association for Counseling and Development, 1991), 9.
3. Diane Langberg, quoted from a presentation for the TRIP Conference, New York City, Oct. 2001.
4. Aphrodite Matsakis, *I Can't Get Over It: A Handbook for Trauma Survivors* (Oakland, CA: New Harbinger, 1992), 6–7.
5. Ibid., 23–24.
6. Ibid., 10–13.

CHAPTER 7

1. Langberg, TRIP Conference.

2. Brown, *Counseling Victims of Violence,* 22–24.

3. Robert Hicks, *Failure to Scream* (Grand Rapids, MI: Baker, 1996), 46.

4. Raymond B. Flannery, Jr., *Post-Traumatic Stress Disorder* (New York: Crossroad, 1992), 36–37.

5. Terence Monmaney, "For Most Trauma Victims Life Is More Meaningful," *L.A. Times,* Sunday, Oct. 7, 2001, 9. Citing research from Richard Tedeschi, University of North Carolina; Dr. Robert Ursano, Uniformed Services University of the Health Sciences in Bethesda, MD; Dr. Sandra Bloom.

6. Matsakis, *I Can't Get Over It,* 134.

7. Ibid., 15, 153.

8. Ibid., 159.

9. Ibid., 160–163.

10. Ibid., 236.

11. H. Norman Wright, *Will My Life Ever Be the Same?* (Eugene, OR: Harvest House, 2002), chapter 8.

CHAPTER 8

1. Karl A. Slaikeu, *Crisis Intervention: A Handbook for Practice and Research* (Boston: Allyn and Bacon, 1984), 89–90.

2. H. Norman Wright, Baker Books, 1985.

3. H. Norman Wright, Harvest House, 1998.

4. Slaikeu, *Crisis Intervention,* 90–91.

CHAPTER 9

1. Richard F. Berg and Christine McCartney, *Depression and the Integrated Life* (New York: Alta House, 1981), 27.

2. Mitch Golant, Ph.D., and Susan K. Golant, *What to Do When Someone You Love Is Depressed* (New York: Henry Holt and Co., 1996), 90–92.

3. H. Norman Wright, *Winning Over Your Emotions* (Eugene, OR: Harvest House, 1998), 32–33.

4. Ibid., 36.

CHAPTER 10

1. Leonard M. Zunin, MD, and Hilary Stanton Zunin, *The Art of Condolence* (New York: HarperCollins, 1991), adapted, 35–39.

2. Ibid., 38.

3. Robert V. Ozment, *When Sorrow Comes* (Waco, TX: Word Books, 1970), 50.

4. Norman Vincent Peale, *Wonderful Promises* (Carmel, NY: Guideposts, 1983), 32.

5. Phyllis Hobe, *Coping* (Carmel, NY: Guideposts, 1983), 233.

6. Barbara Russell Chesser, *Because You Care* (Waco, TX: Word Books, 1970), 50.

7. Zunin and Zunin, *The Art of Condolence*, 61–62.

8. Ibid., 72–73.

9. Ibid., 97–98.

CHAPTER 11

1. Joyce Rupp, *Praying Our Goodbyes* (Notre Dame, IN: Ave Maria Press, 1988), 79.

2. "And the Father Will Dance." Lyrics adapted from Zephaniah 3:14, 17 and Psalm 54:2, 4. Arranged by Mark Hayes. Used by permission.

3. Dr. Gordon MacDonald. Trauma conference in New York, 2001.

CHAPTER 12

1. Source unknown.

2. Judy Tatelbaum, *The Courage to Grieve* (New York: Harper & Row, 1980), 44.

3. Donna Ewy and Rodger Ewy, *Death of a Dream* (New York: Dutton, 1984), adapted, 80.

4. Wylie, *The Survival Guide for Widows,* 113.

5. Fred Bauer, *Just a Touch of Nearness* (Norwalk, CT: C.R. Gibson Co., 1985), 24–25.

6. Joseph Bayly, *The Last Thing We Talk About* [formerly titled *The View From the Hearse*] (Colorado Springs, CO: Cook Communications, 1969, 1992), 40.

7. Carol Staudacher, *Beyond Grief* (Oakland, CA: New Harbinger Publications, 1987), 230–231.

8. Ibid., 231–232.

9. Lauren Briggs, *What to Say When You Don't Know What to Say* (Eugene, OR: Harvest House Publishers, 1985), adapted, 150–155.